THE GOVERNORS OF TEXAS

BOOKS BY ROSS PHARES

Bible in Pocket, Gun in Hand
Texas Tradition
Cavalier in the Wilderness
Reverend Devil

THE PELICAN GOVERNORS SERIES

The Governors of Louisiana, by Miriam Reeves
The Governors of Alabama, by John Craig Stewart
The Governors of Texas, by Ross Phares
In Preparation
The Governors of Tennessee, by Margaret Phillips
The Governors of Florida, by Martin La Godna and
John TePaske

THE
GOVERNORS
OF
TEXAS

By

Ross Phares

PELICAN PUBLISHING COMPANY

GRETNA 1976

Library of Congress Cataloging in Publication Data

Phares, Ross.
   The Governors of Texas.

   (The Pelican governors series)
   Bibliography.
   Includes index.
   SUMMARY: Short biographies with photos of the gov-
ernors of Texas during its French, Spanish, and Mexican
periods, its interval as a republic, and its statehood.
    1. Texas—Governors—Biography. [1. Texas—Governors—
Biography] 1. Title.
F385.P45   976.4'00992 [B] [920]   76-7013
ISBN 0-88289-078-6

Manufactured in the United States of America

Published by Pelican Publishing Company
630 Burmaster Street, Gretna, Louisiana 70053

Contents

Acknowledgments

Many persons have helped in this work. Appreciation is expressed to living ex-governors, to Governor Dolph Briscoe, Jr., and to members of governors' families who have furnished information.

Acknowledgment of indebtedness for materials provided is due R. W. Norton Art Gallery (library), Shreveport, Louisiana; Shreve-Memorial Library, Shreveport; Texas State Library, Austin; and the Texas Collection, University of Texas Library, Austin. Very special thanks are due Miss Nell Cunningham, Louisiana State University in Shreveport Library, who secured rare source material through loans; Mrs. Elizabeth Wallace, Stephen F. Austin State University Library, Nacogdoches, for her generous assistance; and Mrs. Mary Newell Pape, Houston Public Library, Houston.

Gratitude is expressed to Dr. Joseph Milton Nance, historian, editor, and professor of history, Texas A & M University, for reading the manuscript and for his thoughtful suggestions, but who is in no way responsible for any errors or oversights; Mrs. Penny Claudis, typist par excellence; Mrs. Mary Martin McDowell, who offered constructive suggestions for smoothness of structure; Mrs. Carol J. Carefoot, Texas State Library, Austin, and Mrs. May

Schmidt, Austin Public Library, for assistance in securing photographs.

Acknowledgments for use of photographs of Jones, Davis, Throckmorton, Stevenson, Jester, and Preston Smith are due the Texas State Library, Austin; those of Moody, Allred, Daniel, Briscoe, and Connally were furnished by the subjects or members of their families; the others were furnished by the Chalberg Photo Collection, Austin-Travis County Collection, Austin Public Library.

THE GOVERNORS OF TEXAS

French Period

RENE ROBERT CAVELIER, SIEUR DE LA SALLE
(1685-1687)

On April 9, 1682, Robert Cavelier de La Salle, after traveling down the Mississippi River to its mouth, made one of the largest territorial claims ever proclaimed by an individual. He claimed for France all the land drained by the Mississippi and its tributaries; in effect, all the territory lying between the Appalachian and Rocky Mountains and south of the Great Lakes to the Gulf of Mexico.

La Salle was a man of great strengths and monumental weaknesses. He was ambitious, courageous, intelligent, and energetic, but because he was also arrogant and overbearing he could never inspire loyalty, nor lead. So the vast territories of his discoveries and explorations slipped from him, and, in the end, to his country's rivals.

La Salle was born in Rouen, France, on November 22, 1643. In 1666 he went to Canada and became a fur trader and explorer. He discovered the Ohio and explored the upper Illinois country. Back in France, he secured a title of nobility and a permit for further explorations in the West, the Mississippi Valley in particular.

After descending the Mississippi, La Salle again went

to France to obtain supplies and followers to secure the territories he claimed. He proposed to the king not only to colonize the new territory, but since France and Spain were then at war, also to conquer adjoining Spanish lands, including Mexico. All he asked of the king was a vessel of thirty guns, ammunition, and authority to raise a force of two hundred men in France. Additional troops to conquer New Spain he would recruit from among the savages. Strange promises indeed for a man who had never led troops, or established governments, and who had repeatedly failed at the fur business.

The king furnished him not one vessel but four, along with more than two hundred colonists, thus equipping him for conquest as well as colonization. His first objective was to establish a settlement at the mouth of the Mississippi. Before the fleet was far at sea, La Salle was quarreling with his naval commander, Beaujeu, and it never ended. Most of the men sided with Beaujeu. La Salle's cold, reserved, moody disposition irritated his men, and they all but mutinied under his rigid discipline. He blamed others, particularly Beaujeu, for his "bad luck," including missing the mouth of the Mississippi, obviously never realizing the difference between bad luck and bad judgment.

After landing in the Matagorda Bay area of Texas in 1685, he established Fort Saint Louis, from which he made a series of expeditions to scout for Spaniards to the west, and then to search for the Mississippi. On January 12, 1687, he set out for Canada to secure supplies for his starving colony, and a few weeks later was murdered by his followers.

Even in his blunders, La Salle served his country. In his failures in the fur trade in the North, he blazed the way for settlement and industry. His dream of finding a water route to the sea was sneered at, but he found one. Only a man dazzled by a dream possibly could have sold the king of France on a project of conquering New Spain with an army of savages. His landing unintendedly beyond the Mississippi gave France a claim to present-day Texas. The fact that France did not follow up was not his fault.

La Salle's vast dreams and energy gave promise of setting France off to a head start in North America, but without common sense and compassion he blew his opportunities, and those of France at that time.

SIEUR BARBIER
(1687-1689)

It is through Sieur Barbier that we get our last dim view of the fading prospects of a French colony in Texas. Barbier had come over with La Salle, and on La Salle's departure for Canada to seek help, he placed Barbier in charge of the French colony—as miserable, disappointed, scared, and hungry a group of people as might ever be called a "colony."

When Barbier took command of Fort Saint Louis on January 12, 1687, he had about twenty persons under his command. They included, as best we can calculate, two friars, a priest, a surgeon, seven women and girls, several children, and some soldiers. About all he had left with him was hope—that La Salle would somehow make it through before it was too late, or that by a miracle some tardy ship would arrive with supplies. With unfriendly Indians about, and Spaniards rabidly jealous of any Frenchman who so much as looked toward Texas, no colony ever existed more dangerously.

One of the few things we know about Barbier is that he married while at Fort Saint Louis. One historian says the bride was "one of the maidens recently brought out from France." Other accounts have it that she was a maiden from one of the Indian tribes.

The colony survived only until the spring of 1689. There are two accounts, differing only in detail, of its bloody ending: While the French were engaged in peaceful pursuits along the bay, a large body of Indians fell upon them and murdered all but five, who escaped to the protection of friendly tribes. The other account says the colony was weakened by a smallpox epidemic, and when a large band of Indians asked admittance to the fort they were refused. When a number of the French came out to receive them in a cabin outside the palisade, the savages rushed inside and massacred all except four young people saved by Indian women.

Barbier and his colonists were brave and made the supreme sacrifice for their country. On the basis of this colony, France claimed Texas for more than a century. But France did not follow up on this colonial enterprise. Staying power, as always, prevailed in the end. Barbier and his colonists were casualties of the fickle ambitions of kings, and the unpredictable hazards of savage-filled wildernesses.

2

Spanish Period

DOMINGO TERAN DE LOS RIOS
(1691-1692)

Domingo Teran de los Rios, the first Spanish governor of the newly created province of Texas, was an unhappy, frustrated man from start to finish of his administration. He had no reason to expect this, for he had long proven himself in the king's service. He had already been a governor for over three years—of Sonora and Sinaloa—and had served the king in Peru for twenty years before coming to Mexico in 1681, as deputy to the *consulado* of Sevilla and then as captain of infantry in the Castle of Sevilla.

His commission, dated January 23, 1691, provided a handsome salary of twenty-five hundred pesos a year and a virtually unlimited territory to rule—"Tejas and adjacent regions." He might explore, conquer, and rule all the Gulf Coast to the Atlantic Ocean, for in general he was instructed to get all Frenchmen out of the region and strengthen it so they could not come back.

Alonso de Leon, governor of Coahuila, had already found the ruins of La Salle's fort and burned them and then established the mission of San Francisco de los Tejas, near the present village of Weches in Houston County.

Though De Leon found no colony, the very idea of Frenchmen in the region had the Spaniards in a state of jitters.

Teran seemingly faced all the prospects for glory a man could want. But instead, just about everything bad that could happen to a governor in primitive Texas did. In the first place, he received a force of only fifty soldiers, along with ten missionaries and three lay brothers. He protested to his superiors and to Father Fray Damian Massanet, heading the missionaries, that his force was inadequate, but neither paid any attention to him.

The expedition left Monclova on May 16, 1691, and headed for the mission of San Francisco. On the way they failed to find supplies and reinforcements on the Gulf Coast that were expected by sea. Teran hesitated, saying they were essential, but Father Massanet would not hear this. And he promptly cited royal orders to His Excellency stating that the establishing of missions was the purpose of the expedition and that no action was to be taken without his approval, thus reducing Teran to a mere governor.

So the eternal fly in the administrative ointment was Father Massanet, bent on saving the souls of the savages without delay, come timid, incompetent governors or tomahawks. He was as stubborn and fearless as they came, trusting only in God for protection that the military thought required gunpowder. So it was that the governor spent most of his administration riding over his domain on a poor horse and living in the open, mainly on reduced rations, and much of that Indian fare. He never had a capitol.

The Tejas Indians were not overjoyed at seeing the Spaniards. Bell ringing and incense burning could not take their minds off a strange malady the last Spaniards left, and no amount of gourd rattling and ground stomping by the medicine man could drive it away. Being more visually perceptive than biologically knowledgeable, the medicine man, ironically, diagnosed the malady as the evil effects of holy water rather than any indiscretions of the soldiers. Stealing horses obviously brought them more joy, and the promise of it, than hearing mass.

Seeing the futility of it all, Teran left Father Massanet to his Latin masses and frocked parades, and struck out for the Caddo tribe to see what the French were up to there. He found none. His mood urged him to go home by way of the Red River, but he could not find out if it was navigable, so he plodded back to the Tejas. He told Father Massanet he could stay as long as he wanted to, but he himself was heading back to Mexico. He helped himself to the mission horses over Massanet's screaming protest, saying the Indians would get them if he didn't, which was probably right.

To make a long, disappointing story short, the mission failed miserably. It foretold a heroic, impractical pattern that the zealous, dedicated missionaries could never quite see through. The Spaniards thought that if they could save the souls of the Indians, they would have their support to save Texas from the land-greedy French, but in a century and a half of steadfast missionary effort, not a single Texas tribe was permanently converted to Christianity. The missionaries often used the military as a scapegoat, saying they did not provide adequate protection or that the soldiers did mischief.

Governor Teran was glad to escape any way he could. He made it to Bernardo Bay on March 5, 1692, where he received instructions from the viceroy to explore the Mississippi. He set out for the river but soon abandoned the project, he said, on account of bad weather, and sailed for Veracruz. And that is the last we hear of him in Texas.

His unfavorable report was doubtless the main reason the Spaniards abandoned the missionary effort in East

Texas for the next two decades.

MARTIN DE ALARCON
(1716-1719)

Martin de Alarcon's administration was a parallel in most respects to that of his predecessor. His main tasks were to establish missions and to keep the French in their place—wherever that was. He never had as many supplies and troops as he thought he needed, and like Teran, he had an impatient, touchy priest on his hands who wanted to boss and blame him for all failures.

Another French "invasion" had created renewed frantic effort to settle Texas. In late 1716 rumors in Mexico City made it sound as if the French were running all over the Texas province, doubtless looking for a place to settle. This time the French were invading by land instead of sea. An enterprising French trader named Louis Juchereau de St. Denis had established the French on the Red River at Natchitoches in 1714, and by mid-1716 had established trade with the Indians and Spaniards as far into the interior as the Rio Grande. After an interview with the viceroy in Mexico, he was employed as a guide to lead an expedition of Spaniards back east and establish them at Los Adaes, fifteen miles west of the French post at Natchitoches, for purpose of trade, from his point of view.

Alarcon was commissioned governor of "Tejas and such other lands as he might conquer" on December 8, 1716. With him came Father Antonio de San Buenaventura Olivares in charge of the religious. The records of the missionaries give one the idea that they were coming back to Christianize the Indians anyway, whether the French were there or not. But it was French incursions that roused the civil authorities to counteraction.

Olivares was old and impatient to get on with his work before it was too late. He was at San Juan Bautista by May 3, disgusted and complaining that the Ramon family in command there was "more interested in smuggling" than furnishing him supplies, and calling for Governor Alarcon to get on with his assignment. Alarcon finally arrived August 3, 1717. He agreed with Olivares about French smuggling, but that was about all. They had started a never-ending quarrel over prerogatives and the governor's slowness.

By May, 1718, the Spaniards had founded a mission to be known as San Antonio de Valero and the Villa de Bejar. But to Olivares' disappointment, the Indians would not congregate. To try to stop the priest's growling and putting the blame on him, the governor said that if he wanted them in such a hurry he saw no way he could provide them other than to round them up with the sword. Bickering turned to insult when Olivares informed both the governor and the viceroy that he considered such methods stupid.

Alarcon at last arrived at the East Texas missions in November, 1718. The Indians had built a thatched hut for receiving the governor. They lifted him into it ceremoniously, fed him choice nuts and fruit, and danced about the old man with great animation, doubtless coached by the missionaries. The governor promptly wrote his superiors that the Indians were overjoyed to see him, which reveals that Father Olivares, though impetuous, knew something about politics, governors, and Indians.

At this time the Indians were almost destitute. They knew the governor had grain and trinkets in the bundles on his pack animals. Time was to prove they were much more uplifted by the sight of corn than the smell of incense, and took more comfort in gunpowder to protect themselves against their earthly enemies than in holy water to protect them against the devil.

Alarcon spent his time riding from mission to mission acting as godfather at baptisms, making long speeches to the Indians on the wonders of Spain and salvation, while they waited patiently for food and trinkets at the end. He wrote lengthy, monotonous reports to the viceroy on statistics of baptisms, number of friendly Indians under his jurisdiction, his desire to expand the dominion of the king, and his need for more troops to do it.

Having one concept of glory, he announced he was ready to drive the French from Natchitoches. The missionaries set off a loud protest. Did His Excellency not know that St. Denis himself, the commandant at Natchitoches, established the Spanish at Los Adaes? The French controlled the Indians on both sides of the border. They often lived with the Indians and married among them, while the Spanish missionary system was patronizing segregation in the extreme. The Indians appreciated the difference and responded in kind. Rile St. Denis and he might chase the whole lot of them back across the Rio Grande.

Considering Alarcon's experience, his subjects expected better of him. A soldier of fortune, he had seen service at Oran, and had been in the royal navy and a captain of infantry at Valencia. In Mexico he held numerous distinguished positions, such as *alcalde mayor* of Tacona and Zamora, protector of Indians at Mazapil, and governor of Coahuila.

Alarcon saw the futility of many of his and the missionaries' efforts, and frustration plagued him. Old, tired, confused, disgusted, he told the missionaries so, as politely as his temper would permit, then wrote a letter of resignation to the viceroy in early 1719.

His resignation was promptly accepted, but it seems nothing ever worked out on schedule for Alarcon. He was kept in office until December. And for the next four years he fretted with officials, trying to collect part of his salary and expense account, until he became bitter as well as bewildered.

In Texas, Alarcon never knew what it was all about, and the missionaries never let him get away with anything they did not approve of.

MARQUES DE SAN MIGUEL DE AGUAYO
(1719-1722)

In mid-1719 an event took place in Texas tailor-made for creating a hero: The French "invaded" Texas and "drove" the Spanish out of the eastern part. Nothing unites people like a common enemy, real or imagined. So the viceroy called up his best pedigreed man to recapture East Texas, a marquis, no less, whose family estate included almost half the state of Coahuila. His ancestors had fought and bled just about everywhere Spanish kings had bloody business to do. He was born in Spain and named Joseph de Azlor. He fought for the king there before coming to Coahuila in 1712. It was through his marriage to an heiress, Ignacia Xaviera, that he gained his title of Marques de Aguayo.

He was appointed governor and captain general of Coahuila and Texas in late 1719 after vowing to drive the French out of any territory claimed by Spain, even to the Mississippi River. Bales of paper have been inked about Aguayo's recapture of Texas and making it forever secure for Spain. Actually, the invasion of 1719 (while France and Spain were at war) was effected by an army of eight men who rode over from Natchitoches and captured a lay brother, one ragged soldier, a flock of chickens, and the ornaments and fixtures of the mission. Fluttering of the chickens spooked the commander's horse and it threw him. In the confusion, the lay brother escaped and ran across Texas crying "the French are coming" so loudly that every cautious Spaniard fled to San Antonio or farther south.

Aguayo marched across the Rio Grande with the largest force ever to enter Texas, about five hundred men, along with four thousand horses and other livestock. He reached San Antonio on April 4, 1721.

At the end of July, Aguayo met St. Denis waiting for him at the Neches River. Much propaganda has been written about this meeting. The Spaniards reported, in effect, that Aguayo, finding St. Denis without his reported army of Indians, told him if he would go quietly back to the Red River he wouldn't attack, at least not then. Pure rubbish! The Frenchman did not need Indians assembled. Just the fact that they were squatting in the brush all over the territory with St. Denis there was enough to scare the daylights out of any knowledgeable Spaniard.

Actually, St. Denis was there to welcome his customers back. He had just been granted a five percent commission on profits of merchandise sold to foreigners. He was glad to see so many of them. He apologized to Aguayo for that misunderstanding about a few of his men riding over to Los Adaes while he was away and the undue fright it caused. His Lordship was flabbergasted at such poise.

St. Denis rode back to Natchitoches. Aguayo brought his expedition to Los Adaes, reestablished the mission, and laid out a presidio. A few days after his arrival, St. Denis rode over to welcome him, bringing chickens for the governor's table along with melons and fresh vegetables. So the two commanders exchanged views, food, and liquor, and there was the crackle of charming conversation rather than exploding gunpowder. Aguayo wrote the viceroy that he had cleared Texas of all Frenchmen, and that there would be no trade with them. At the time, Aguayo's troops were living on bread made from French corn, and

St. Denis ordered more drygoods.

Aguayo's expedition has been grossly overrated. He did not gain a single foot of territory for Spain, and he did not stop French trade. He simply led the Spaniards back without opposition to the place they had run away from, and now both the French and Spanish were where they had been before the "invasion."

Aguayo resigned in 1722, giving as reason ill health resulting from the hardships of the expedition. In 1724 he was given the rank of field marshal by the king. He died March 7, 1734, and was buried in the chapel of Santa Maria de las Parras. The Texas expedition had brought Aguayo no glory, just fatigue and great expense.

FERNANDO PEREZ DE ALMAZAN
(1722-)

Fernando Perez de Almazan got the governorship of Texas mainly because he happened to be in the right place at the right time. And he held onto it longer than the average, doubtless because he had on-the-spot experience and had made some practical observations. He was lieutenant governor under Aguayo. When Aguayo, tired, sick, and outwitted by the French, threw in the towel in early 1722 and headed back toward Coahuila, he left Almazan in charge.

The best firsthand information about him comes from Aguayo's recommendation to the viceroy. He said no one was better able to carry out the "reorganization" of the province than Don Fernando, "whose noble parentage, distinguished services, unquestioned ability, unselfish devotion to duty, and great zeal" fitted him particularly for the position of governor. He said that he was well liked by the Indians, the soldiers had a high opinion of him, and the missionaries looked upon his possible appointment with favor.

If any governor ever knew what to do right off, he should have. He had seen how Aguayo had worn himself out trying to prevent trade with the French while the Spanish population grew hungrier and more ragged. So he enforced no restrictions. The viceroy, in time, got wind of this and called his hand. The governor pleaded in response that due to crop failures, the long distances, and delays in transportation, the Spanish would suffer without trade. And the French had no priest at Natchitoches, so Spanish priests officiated there. The two nationalities helped each other. He was one of the few Spanish governors ever bold enough to tell a viceroy he thought it was a pretty good arrangement.

The viceroy promptly put his foot down on this, and Almazan replied that all intercourse between the two nations would cease at once. But there was no way for this distant wilderness outpost to live entirely alone, and he knew it.

His disillusionment increased as he rode over his province from post to post. As a rule he found them undersupplied, undermanned, and incompetently administered, the Indians refusing to take to the plow and prayers, rebelling against congregating, and going on the warpath in some instances; the Apaches were especially troublesome. He had rafts built to ferry supplies, but when there were supplies the streams always seemed too high to cross.

In 1726 and 1727 he repeatedly wrote to the viceroy that he was sick, tired of his job, and wanted to quit. When the viceroy did nothing about it, he at last took matters into his own hands and appointed Melchor Mediavilla, captain of Los Adaes, as lieutenant governor. Mediavilla served as chief administrative officer in Texas probably more than three years, but the viceroy never sanctioned his appointment. Thus historians do not list him as a true governor.

The records are in conflict about the terminal date of Almazan's tenure. He spent some time in San Antonio and was in Mexico City by 1729. It seems that when he could not get officially relieved, he just rode off from the capitol at Los Adaes toward Mexico and slipped quietly out of the province.

JUAN ANTONIO BUSTILLO Y ZEVALLOS
(1731-1734?)

Juan Antonio Bustillo y Zevallos, the most practical-minded, youthful, and possibly the most cultured governor of Texas up to his time, was brave in the face of both Indians and viceroys. He added both the light touch and efficiency to Texas politics, diplomacy, and commerce. He came from one of the best-known and most cultured families of Spain, in the mountains of Burgos, and was a nobleman with the rank of *hildago*.

By the spring of 1725 he was commandant at La Bahia. When Rivera inspected the post, he reported it as the most efficiently administered in the province and recommended Bustillo for governor. Date of his commission is not certain, but he arrived at the Los Adaes capital April 28, 1731, driving ahead of him several hundred head of livestock and bringing probably the most supplies the post had ever seen at one time. By his own statement he was forty years old and had seen eight years of service in the province.

The French commandant at Natchitoches, St. Denis, knew of him and his coming. St. Denis' wife was a member of a ruling family in Mexico, and what the Indians didn't tell him about doings in Texas, his wife's relatives usually did. St. Denis called on him immediately. The meeting may have determined the immediate course of Louisiana-Texas history. Both of these cultured men were probably starved for charming conversation, and over Bustillo's best wine and food they became fast friends.

Bustillo reported to the viceroy that trade existed with the French, mainly in such minor items as vegetables, but all was closely supervised, and that the surrounding Indians were well supplied with French guns and about everything else they wanted. In this light he subtly suggested to His Excellency that the French commandant was not an appropriate man to antagonize, about trade or anything else.

In this year of his arrival, the Natchez Indians were threatening to wipe out the Louisiana colony. After overrunning most of Louisiana, they attacked Natchitoches on October 5. A few hours later an excited horseman dashed up to the Spanish capitol on a sweat-soaked horse with an urgent message from St. Denis to the governor to seek aid. Bustillo might have thought of old scores to settle and reasoned that if the Natchez destroyed the French, it would be Spain's long-awaited opportunity to push across to the Mississippi, join Texas and Florida together, and make the Gulf of Mexico a Spanish sea. But this was an appeal from a friend, and he replied as such. He dispatched Spanish soldiers and a contingent of Indian allies to Louisiana, and for twenty-two days the two nationalities fought side by side. One Spanish soldier was killed. Louisiana was saved.

Bustillo was noted mostly for settling Canary Islanders in San Antonio in 1731, and personally leading a successful campaign against the Apaches in 1732 that brought temporary peace. Just when he ended his governorship is not certain; it was probably 1734. He became an *alcalde ordinario* of Mexico City, and in 1751 was a member of the *Audiencia*, the highest administrative and judicial body of New Spain.

The frontier had done better than usual under Bustillo. Evidently his exercise of common sense, sometimes at variance with royal orders, and his friendship with the French commandant did him no political harm.

MANUEL DE SANDOVAL
(1734-1736)

Manuel de Sandoval was commissioned governor of Texas in early 1734, and from then on he had little peace of mind. Even at fighting the Indians, his specialty, he had but limited success; and all the old problems of the eastern frontier rose up to haunt him, along with a few new ones.

A native of Santa Fe, New Mexico, he joined the army there and rose slowly in twenty years from cadet to captain of the local grenadiers. He served as governor of Coahuila from 1727 to 1734. He came to Texas partly because the viceroy thought that as a military man he could put down the warring Apaches. But nobody at that time, it appears, could do that—at least not for long.

The Indians kept him occupied away from his capitol, from which he heard nothing but complaints. The whole establishment was rotting, the crops had failed, the main prospects for food were from the French, and they had raised their prices out of reach. Sandoval, because of age and weariness, may not have been as alert and as successful at personal defense as a younger and better-educated man might have been. But the way his luck was running, about every molehill of a mistake or reverse flared into a volcanic mountain.

As if the food problems, warring Indians, and tumbling-down capitol were not troubles enough for the absentee governor, the French chose this critical moment to move their fort a short distance to the west, a mere few feet, but it definitely established the French on the west side of the Red River. Nothing in eighteenth-century Texas inspired as much writing. Sandoval, new in Texas and knowing no more than had recently been told him, set out to defend the Spanish side of the boundary dispute. St. Denis, who had been there long before there was a boundary, got the best of the argument. Both sides threatened war.

Sandoval not only faced unsolvable problems, but he was a continued victim of ruinous timing of events. While caught between the warring Apaches and the "invading" French, and prodded by the viceroy to get things straightened out on both sides of his province, there appeared in Mexico City in 1736 one Carlos Franquis de Lugo with a commission from the king for the governorship of Tlaxcala. But that office was filled, and Franquis had to be taken care of without delay. So in view of some bad reports on Sandoval, he was chosen as loser.

As soon as Franquis had his commission changed to the governorship of Texas, he stormed into the province and arrested Sandoval on sight without a warrant, and put him in stocks in front of his capitol for everybody to gape at. To humiliation, Franquis added charges of misconduct against Sandoval for not residing at Los Adaes, not keeping his books properly, reducing the missionaries, and conniving with the French. On the first charge he was fined five hundred pesos, though he was busy fighting the Indians beyond San Antonio at the time.

There were countersuits, but in the end Sandoval was bankrupted and sent to prison. Official investigation of the Sandoval case and previous happenings in Texas filled seventy volumes. The material was used in later boundary negotiations between Spain, France, and the United States. Thomas Jefferson, among others, studied them in search of the true western boundary of Louisiana.

As might be surmised, politics was at the bottom of this whole troublesome business. In December, 1743, a new viceroy in favor of Sandoval exonerated him. He was released from prison and again given a position in the army, where he served until his death. He doubtless would have lived a much happier life if he had never left the army.

CARLOS FRANQUIS DE LUGO
(1736-1737)

Carlos Franquis de Lugo might have realized his ambition to get rich in Texas if he had talked less, and taken his time.

Born in the Canary Islands in 1691, obviously of people of little substance, he moved to Havana, Cuba, in early manhood, where he married Angela de Alarcon. He blew into Texas like a whirlwind in 1736 without formal announcement or showing his governor's commission, insulting, ignoring, and bulldozing officials on his hasty journey to the frontier to put Sandoval and the French in their places. If Sandoval had let the French push him around, he deserved what he was getting. He announced that he would not only put the French back on the "right side" of the Red River, but he might even run them all the way across the Mississippi if they trifled with him. He had heard that Governor Sandoval was a wealthy man, a point that interested him exceedingly. But instead of talking business, he arrested him on sight.

Like most smart alecks, Franquis did more talking than thinking. While he was loudly threatening and boasting, St. Denis quietly rode over from Natchitoches and told him the French were there to stay, just where they were, and

His Excellency could save himself a lot of pains if he forgot all about the boundary. The country by now looked so poor that Franquis decided Sandoval had gotten his money somewhere else. Also there appeared no point to him in risking fortune and glory by tangling with a stubborn Frenchman over a fragment of land. He took the commandant's advice.

He thundered back into the interior, and turned his fiery, abusive energy to suppressing and making fun of the missionaries and minor civil officials. He had dreams of military grandeur, so he called for more troops to lead, telling how he would annihilate certain unconquerable tribes. But his dreams of military glory faded out at the more practical and safer idea that live Indians might be worth more to him than dead ones. Instead of putting them to the sword, he would put them to the plow. This could have a double advantage, he thought. He could use both the Indians and troops in productive enterprises—a type of reasoning that showed him not to be as stupid as some of his critics claimed.

But enemies grew faster and thicker around him than crops and commerce. How much he made by exploiting the Indians and settlers is impossible to say, but certainly time robbed him of any great fortune, for on July 9, 1737, he was arrested for overbearing conduct. One historian said that in a little more than a year Franquis came to very nearly ruining the entire province, doing more harm than the continuing attacks of the implacable Apaches.

After a trial lasting several years, and lawsuits involving Sandoval, Franquis became an officer of the garrison of Vera Cruz and eventually saw service in the regiment of Savoya in Spain, where he died. Ever lacking in patience and tact, both his coveted riches and glory eluded him to the last.

JOSEPH FERNANDEZ DE JAUREGUI Y URRUTIA
(1737)

Joseph Fernandez de Jauregui had an extraordinary title and function in Texas. On July 11, 1737, he was appointed governor extraordinary and *visitador* of Texas, and his chief assigned function was to investigate Franquis. At that time he was governor and captain general of Nuevo Leon. But with two ex-governors, Franquis and Sandoval, in a political dogfight, somebody was desperately needed to bring the province out of chaos.

The friendly mission Indians, exploited by Franquis, were running away. Thus the missionaries were virtually out of business, and defenseless, too, with the allied natives gone and the soldiers away fighting Apaches. There was nobody at home to fight or administer. It was as if Texas was in a runaway wagon with no hands on the reins.

Jauregui started his investigation in September. Day after day he listened to all kinds of charges, but one defender called Franquis "noble, generous" and said he was regarded "like legendary heroes of antiquity, not as a mere man." Jauregui must have realized that the Franquis-Sandoval cloud would hang over the land for a long time, ultimately to fade like disturbing ghosts into the mist of opinion. He concluded his report to the viceroy by October 15, and appointed Don Prudencio de Orobio y Basterra in charge of government affairs. He gave as his reason for a hasty departure the need to put down an Indian uprising in Nuevo Leon.

Doubtless Jauregui realized there was little he could do for Texas or the individuals concerned. He submitted reams of testimony, but higher officials and courts could take it from there. Like most other governors before him, he was glad to be gone.

PRUDENCIO DE OROBIO Y BASTERRA
(1737-1741)

Prudencio de Orobio y Basterra was one of the few businessmen appointed governor of Texas. Governor Jauregui hurriedly appointed him governor *ad interim* about mid-October, 1737, so he could get back to his Indian fighting in Nuevo Leon.

Because he was a vague character for a governor, we pick up Orobio's story mainly through footnotes to history. He seems to have at one time been commander at the La Bahia presidio, and *alcalde mayor* of Parras, Coahuila. But mainly he was a businessman—a trader in Saltillo and owner of a cattle and horse ranch at present-day Mier.

As governor he appears to have attended to his own business, literally and figuratively, while Texas drifted. Seeming without grasp or initiative for concerted action, he authorized campaigns against the Apaches either prematurely or too late, missionary reports indicate, irritating the Apaches more than quelling them. He managed to conduct trade with the French in produce, but the settlers complained it was too little and not for the right items. When he heard that the French were trading on the lower Trinity, or maybe attempting settlement, he sent an expedition to find out. It got lost. Hearing of the French being up to something here and there in other parts of the province, he chased them as if they were a will-o'-the-wisp, until he decided they were merely trying to make a few pesos at trade—about like every other civilian in the woods.

His term was over by 1741. He left Texas just about as he found it.

THOMAS FELIPE WINTUISEN
(1741-1743)

Thomas Felipe Wintuisen became governor of Texas in 1741. Because there seems to be no account of him in the military records, it is supposed he was a civilian. We know very little about him. Texas had become comparatively quiet during this period, so the records are relatively few. The officials at Mexico City obviously considered the eastern frontier relatively stabilized from the standpoints of boundaries and trade, though nothing was actually settled. The Indians were peaceful there—better this way, under control of the French, than out of control under their own attemped management.

The missionaries plodded on their slow, discouraging way, pleading for more protection and complaining of the natives' lack of enthusiasm for mission life, but ever ambitious and brimming full of faith to the point that they contended they could tame the Apaches with the story of Christ's love where the soldiers were failing with gunpowder. During Wintuisen's term the Apaches continued to raid San Antonio, and the Comanches appeared with warpaint in the north.

Nothing really worked during this period. All hands merely endured. In 1743 Wintuisen faded out of office as quietly and mysteriously as he had come in, and history books do not even carry his name.

JUSTO BONEO Y MORALES
(1743-1744)

Justo Boneo y Morales rode into office on the backlash of the old Franquis-Sandoval controversy. There seemed no end to it, for the mills of justice ground exceedingly finely and slowly in old Mexico.

Boneo was of high rank, a knight of the Order of Santiago and a lieutenant colonel in the Spanish army. On July 15, 1740, he was ordered to investigate the boundary between the Spanish and French and the charges made by Franquis against Sandoval and the missionaries of Texas. Just when Boneo started his investigation and where he spent his time are not clear. He probably spent months pouring over the seventy volumes written specifically about the Franquis-Sandoval case and the related history of the province, probably in Mexico City. Then there were other innumerable documents, for just about everybody of any importance in the government, army, and church had written something about this complicated affair, from one side or the other.

On December 17, 1743, Boneo was at Los Adaes working on his investigation when he received his appointment as governor of Texas. News, like justice, took a slow course in those days—the viceroy had written the appointment a year and two days earlier. Boneo's investigation up to this time seems to have boiled down to the conclusion that it was impossible to determine from the evidence where the boundary should be between the Spanish and French. By this time no one could get any clear view of the proverbial forest for the ever-increasing details of trees.

He was not governor long enough to do much about anything on the frontier. Seemingly the most encouraging occurrence during his administration, from a Spanish viewpoint, was the death of St. Denis on June 11, 1744. Boneo and other Spanish dignitaries rode over from their Spanish capitol to Natchitoches to attend the funeral. A few days later Boneo reported the occurrence to the viceroy in language that said, in effect: "St. Denis is dead now. Thank God, we can breathe easier."

If there were new prospects at St. Denis' death of a

shift to stronger Spanish influence and less French inter-
ference on the frontier, Boneo did not live to see it. He
died in September, 1744, the labors of another career on
the frontier merely adding repetitious bulk to the mount-
ing pile of memorabilia that changed nothing significantly
or gave much hope of it.

FRANCISCO GARCIA LARIOS
(1744-1748)

Francisco Garcia Larios became governor of Texas on
the death of Justo Boneo y Morales in September, 1744.
Little is known of his life before or after his governorship.
Spain was becoming disillusioned and paying less attention
to its governors and their situations in the Texas province.
The province was a drain on the royal treasury and recognized by now as not likely to show a profit, at least not in
the foreseeable future. The missionaries were bickering
with the military and civil officials about how to handle
the Indians—saving the Indian's soul while saving their own
scalps. French traders appeared unstoppable among the
Texas tribes.

So Larios was mainly engaged in arguing with the missionaries, primarily about their proposed establishments
on the San Xavier River, which he stubbornly contended
were impractical and indefensible. The missionaries per-
suaded the viceroy they were right, and Larios lost the
argument. But the controversy was the chief subject of
the documents of his administration, and like most Texas
colonial arguments, it lasted on and on.

In 1747 he proposed to explore personally the Gulf
Coast as far south as the Rio Grande—among other objec-
tives, it seems, to investigate possibilities of establishing
settlements and to chase out any French traders he found

doing business there. But in the end this was left to a sub-
ordinate, and like about everything else we know about
Larios' administration, it boiled down to a lot of talk and
spreading of ink, and little significant action.

He is listed in some accounts as *ad interim* governor.
Whatever his exact status, it was over by mid-1748.

PEDRO DEL BARRIO JUNCO Y ESPRIELLA
(1748-1750)

Just as it appeared affairs were getting dull and routine, Pedro del Barrio Junco y Espriella became governor
and stirred up the Texas province like nothing else since
the old Franquis-Sandoval mess. He was appointed governor *ad interim* June 3, 1748. He immediately locked
horns with the missionaries over their efforts to locate establishments on the San Xavier (San Gabriel) River. He,
like Governor Larios, lost the argument, which seems to
have done his temper no good when dealing with other
people in Texas.

Barrio made more than one personal inspection and
report of San Xavier to support his stand that the location
was impractical and indefensible. He reported that the
soldiers there were deeply discouraged over defeats by the
Indians, who also stole their horses; in the rainy season the
river overflowed, and in dry weather it dried up; the natives congregated there not to hear about Christ but for
protection against the Apaches and for trade, including
that with the French.

The missionaries went all the way to Mexico City to
argue against the governor. Barrio, who was notable as a
gambling man, wagered his head that the mission would
not be maintained on the San Xavier. The missionaries, of
course, never attempted to collect on such a wager, but

they took advantage of a fitting figure of speech to proclaim that in their opinion the governor had already lost his head.

When the viceroy went against him, he seems to have taken his superior's other judgments and decrees with as little respect. He lifted all bans on gambling and engaged in trade with the French. At least the missionaries said he did, and they finally got an investigation started against him, referred to in history books as the "introduction of an unsavory chapter in Texas history."

Barrio brooked no support of the Xavier matter by his officials. When Toribio Urrutia, long-time captain of San Antonio, signed a document in this connection supporting the missionaries' stand, Barrio upbraided him sharply, saying he was more in need of his sword than his pen, and apparently sent him to jail to meditate over his "insubordination and meddling."

One may wonder on casual observation why Barrio landed in Texas in a stew and stayed in it virtually the whole of his administration. He could hardly have been against the missionary program per se, for he had been the *alcalde provincial* of the Santa Hermandad of all New Spain, a holy brotherhood; he had previous administrative experience, as governor of Neuvo Leon for six years; and he should have understood Indians (which may have caused in part his objection to San Xavier), for he had led numerous campaigns against them. As a military man he obviously had ability, when under control, for as late as March 27, 1765, he was appointed captain of Paso del Norte.

Obviously the overzealous set-in-their-way missionaries and minor officials irritated him, and he chose to stand like a mighty oak in the wind, too stiff to sway, and the storm broke him. He was removed from the governorship in late 1750—to the last, too stiff a timber to bend at all.

JACINTO DE BARRIOS Y JAUREGUI
(1751-1759)

By the time Jacinto de Barrios y Jauregui was appointed governor and captain general of Texas in 1751, the power struggle between the missionaries and the governorship had become something of a tradition. The struggle had been intense and constant during his predecessor's administration, and the stage was set for him to continue the drama—which he did, from start to finish.

The missionaries said Barrios knew too many intimate details about the missions, particularly San Xavier, for a stranger, that his opinions were fixed from talk with previous governors residing in Mexico City before he reached the province. By the time he arrived at his capitol at Los Adaes in June, he had left a long trail of irritated priests already buzzing about the inkpots eager to furnish complaints and opinions to their superiors. They even made some play on the similarity of his and his predecessor's name and character—that he was a Barrio in the plural. They wrote, among other things, that he had slighted the missionaries, made violent threats against them, planned to put the Indians to work for the Canary Islanders, was withdrawing military support, and had in particular abused Father Fray Joseph Pinilla "in a manner unbecoming his birth and rank and the character of the religious," and so on and so on.

A military career man, Barrios had entered the service of the Spanish king about 1718 and rose from ensign to lieutenant colonel in campaigns against the Italians. He came to New Spain with a commission from the king. (*Ad interim* governors might be appointed by the viceroy.) A royal appointee such as Barrios was usually governor and captain general of his province and captain of the presidio of Los Adaes, the capital. In this capacity he exercised both civil and military authority.

If we believe the reports of the missionaries, Barrios was one of the most corrupt of governors by virtue of his operating a monopoly of foreign trade. Certainly he did engage in trade, and probably made a modest fortune at it, particularly among the Orcoquiza and Bidai. He bought goods at Natchitoches, such as knives, scissors, even fire-arms, and transported them in pack trains under guard of soldiers and traded them for such items as deer and buffalo hides. He also sold to soldiers and civilians at Los Adaes and Saltillo.

Aside from his extensive business ventures, he had a hand in other notable occurrences—the founding of San Agustin de Ahumada, moving of the San Xavier missions and San Francisco Xavier presidio to the San Marcos River, recommending the expedition against the Apaches by Diego Ortiz Parilla, and founding of the mission of San Saba de la Santa Cruz and the San Saba presidio. And he, like most other governors of this period, was ordered to in-vestigate the eastern boundary, which he did in 1753. He reported that the Red River was the true boundary, but testimony showed that since 1736 the Arroyo Hondo, about midway between Los Adaes and Natchitoches, was the accepted limit. He reported that the Spanish were at the mercy of the French, that in case of war (apparently thinking of the Indians) they could massacre all the Spanish.

He made efforts to keep the French out of the prov-ince, especially along the Trinity River—possibly both as an official duty and to keep down competition for his business. And like numerous other governors, he had mines to investigate. In 1755 reports abounded of silver mines in the Llano and upper Colorado regions, mountains of pure silver. One reporter stated that the mines of Cerro del Almagre were so numerous that he could guarantee a mine for each inhabitant in the entire province—as usual, much more exciting talk than precious metal.

In mid-1756 Angel de Martos y Navarrete was appointed governor of Texas and Barrios governor of Coahuila, but the appointments were interchanged to permit Barrios to remain in Texas until 1759 to complete the founding of the presidio of San Agustin de Ahumada.

Evidently neither his trade with the French nor the tattling of the missionaries did him any real political damage. After leaving Texas, Barrios served two terms as governor of Coahuila.

ANGEL DE MARTOS Y NAVARRETE
(1759-1766)

Angel de Martos y Navarrete might well be called the vagabond governor of Texas. He survived primarily, it seems, by virtue of uncanny luck and/or sufficient habitual inertia to let time take care of his problems, such as they were taken care of. His contemporaries complained that he lived like an Indian in his capital, letting both equipment and morale go to pot. He was accused, probably correctly, of making a profit of a thousand percent on illegal foreign goods sold to his garrison. He used the labor of the soldiers to operate his farm and stock ranch, and sanctioned a campaign against the northern Indians that resulted in a rout and a "disgrace to Spanish arms." In the end he was found guilty of burning a town.

Martos was a naval lieutenant before receiving his royal commission as governor on August 26, 1756. Even in the beginning, time was kind to him, for his predecessor was allowed to remain in Texas to carry out some projects already under way. So Martos acted as governor of Coahuila until February 6, 1759, while some of the most troublesome problems of Texas were diminished.

Actually, the disastrous campaign against the northern Indians led by Diego Ortiz Parilla was pretty well set
by his predecessor. Martos merely nodded his approval,
which was about as much action as he took on many
official duties. His actions concerning location of missions on the lower Trinity are typical. He seems to have
done as little as possible and let problems wait and fizzle
out. Such was the handling of the proposed removal of
Los Horconsitos. The governor changed his mind a time
or two and ended up by asking the viceroy to relieve him
of the responsibility. Typically, nothing was done. His
conflicts with the missionaries were mild. He simply let
them talk and wear the issues out without aggravating
them.

In 1763 he got into a boundary dispute—doubtless
pressed into it by his superiors—with Chevalier Macarty,
commandant of Natchitoches, over the eastern boundary.
He had the most troublesome of defenses on his hands, for
Macarty claimed that by virtue of La Salle's colony,
France had a valid claim to all territory lying east of a line
running north of the Bay of San Louis. But Martos' luck
was still holding. Already Louisiana had been ceded to
Spain, though the cession of 1762 was not known on the
border. So the boundary and contraband trade were beginning to lose their political significance, and time again
temporarily settled the issues.

Martos' luck could not endure forever. In November,
1763, Rafael Martinez Pacheco was appointed commander
of the San Agustin de Ahumada presidio. Charges against
him by his troops brought Martos to the presidio to investigate. When Martos ordered the commander's arrest, he
barricaded himself in the presidio, and a shoot-out resulted. After several days of a standoff, soldiers set fire to
the presidio to rout out Pacheco. He escaped, and so, it

seems, did Martos' luck in the affair. Martos, accused of responsibility for burning the presidio, could not shake off the charge. In this instance, time did not work in his favor. In typical Spanish fashion, the investigation and trial dragged on for fourteen years. In the end he was found guilty and assessed a heavy fine, but by the end of 1766 it was all over for him as governor.

This ruinous Pacheco affair seems out of character for Martos. He did not appear a violent man; he was always ready to sway rather than risk breaking. He had such a good thing going for him—enormously profitable trade and other personal enterprises—that it does not seem he would have risked rocking the political boat so recklessly. But time and luck eventually run out on all men.

HUGO OCONOR
(1767-1770)

Hugo Oconor, unlike other governors up to his time, influenced major events in Texas before and after his administration. He was also different, in degree at least, from his recent predecessors—he was popular, dedicated to official duties, and possessed noticeable administrative ability. Yet circumstantial evidence indicates he may have been a man of far-reaching human weakness.

He was probably Irish by birth. His flaming red hair caused the Indians to call him the "Red Captain." As inspector general for frontier Spain, he came to San Agustin to investigate the trouble between Governor Martos and Pacheco. The records indicate that Martos deserved to be fired as governor on general principles, but considering the manner of his firing, there is room to wonder about the purity of Oconor's motives.

It seems that Martos was not at San Agustin at the

time of the burning of the presidio, and that Marcos Ruiz,
commander of government troops, was first arrested for
the offense. Martos unfortunately had few personal assets
in his favor for winning approval and respect. He was
sloppy, careless, without poise, dull—no match for Oconor
in such respects. Oconor, according to Governor Martos,
arrived at San Agustin accompanied by a cousin of
Pacheco; and primarily, if not entirely, on the basis of
Oconor's investigation and report, he got Martos' job as
governor in 1767.

Oconor's administration is described as efficient and
energetic. He reorganized and strengthened the garrison at
San Antonio, increased order in government in general,
checked temporarily the ravages of the northern tribes,
and chastised the raiding Apaches.

After leaving the governorship of Texas in 1770, he
was promoted from the rank of sergeant major to colonel
and in time became commandant inspector of the Internal
Provinces. In this position Oconor still had the upper hand
in Texas, and again there is reason to suspect human weakness showing through his official armor—which gets ahead
of our story of governors. When the succession of 1762 became known, orders were sent out to abandon the presidios of East Texas, as they were no longer needed to guard
a frontier. The Baron de Ripperda had become governor
and listened to the petition of the settlers of Los Adaes to
remain at their homes, and he so recommended. Oconor
opposed. There was jealousy and hatred between the two
men. Ripperda appealed to the viceroy over Oconor's
head, pointing out that he was his senior in rank, age, and
length of service, and asked if he had to obey him. Oconor
heard about this, and the feud became bitter. Oconor even
had Antonio Gil Ybarbo, leader of the Adaesians, imprisoned.

Certainly, from humane and practical standpoints,

Ripperda was in the right, and it was later officially so agreed. Oconor demonstrated that ability and dedication do not necessarily preclude self-interest and prejudice.

JUAN MARIA VICENCIO DE RIPPERDA, BARON DE RIPPERDA
(1770-1778)

Baron de Ripperda was a romanticist. A native of Madrid and a nobleman, he grew up amid the excitement, finery, and comforts of the glittering capital of old Spain, where he heard talk of the ever-expanding empire. He in time dreamed of having a part in it—commanding armies, ruling loyal, obedient subjects, bringing civilization and Christianity to adoring simple natives in strange wilderness lands, and winning the admiration of his king. So in early 1769 he hit the glory trail for Texas to become governor. The stage was indeed set for high drama for this romantic, but it was all tragic drama.

The dashing baron had one final fling at gaiety in the New World. While waiting in Mexico City for the administration of Oconor to end, he fell in love with and married, on October 22, 1769, a beautiful heiress, Dona Mariana Gomez de Parada. In March of the following year the baron and his bride were in San Antonio, now the temporary capital. The best lodging they could find was an abandoned calaboose, and his capitol was a mere shack, "in ruins." His orders for improvement brought no results. The citizens had little respect for governors, being mainly engrossed in saving their scalps from raiding Indians. In this dilapidated one-room jail, the young baroness gave birth to her first child.

Ripperda's chief concern was the Indians. He had to use threats to keep citizens from abandoning San Antonio from fear of marauders. He called for reinforcements from other presidios, and this brought missionaries down on him from all sides, saying he was risking ruin to the mission system. Then fears of an English attack swept over the province.

In 1772 the capital of Texas was officially moved to San Antonio. The next year orders came to Ripperda to remove the East Texas establishments back into the interior, now that there was no frontier to guard. One might think that in the cession of Louisiana to Spain, the French would have felt the impact most. They did complain that their king had dealt lightly with them, but their miseries were light compared with those of the Spanish of East Texas, who wailed that they were being treated brutally by being removed. Los Adaes was the only home most of them knew, and many had married into French families.

Governor Ripperda came to Los Adaes hoping he could prevent the abandonment, but Oconor opposed him and he went away in deep disappointment. The Adaesians were told to prepare to march in five days. The aged Lieutenant Governor Gonzales, on orders, rode through the streets with a whip in hand driving the people from their homes, a task that broke his heart. He died a few days later in Nacogdoches. This incident reminds one of the expulsion of the Acadians from Nova Scotia and their wanderings.

The Adaesians died by the scores from hardships. Their leader, Antonio Gil Ybarbo, went to Mexico City, petitioning the viceroy to allow them to return to their homes. Only after six years of wandering were they permitted to return as close as Nacogdoches, where they made a permanent settlement, thus ending an illustrative episode in the fading glory of an out-worn system where the state came first and the people last, and bringing the curtain down on one of Texas' sorriest and most tragic dramas.

One encouraging event in Ripperda's administration was the aid of Athanase de Mezieres in bringing the northern tribes under control. But Oconor beclouded even this by casting suspicion on the work and belittling it, saying the governor favored Frenchmen and engaged in illicit trade. As a result, the viceroy forbade Ripperda all communication with Louisiana, and removed him in 1778 for noncompliance. The disillusioned baron died in October, 1780, as governor of Honduras.

DOMINGO CABELLO
(1778-1786)

Domingo Cabello was a practical man of common sense. He was not lazy, but by often letting well enough alone he maintained better than usual relations with his people.

His record before coming to Texas may be described as efficient, though not brilliant. A native of Castile, Spain, he became a soldier by profession, rising to lieutenant by 1741. In 1762 he was appointed governor of Nicaragua in recognition of his bravery at Havana. He held the rank of colonel when he became governor of Texas in 1778.

Cabello listened with patience to the missionaries, was firm with them in his decisions, and in the main was respected by them. He attempted to make himself knowledgeable in detail about conditions in his province, and on September 30, 1784, he submitted a complete report to the commander general of the *Provincias Internas*. He took a census of the Texas missions in 1785, in 1786 he commissioned Pedro Vial to explore a direct route from San Antonio to Santa Fe, and he approved the permanent settlement of the Adaesians at Nacogdoches.

He emphatically declared the Indians could not be

trusted. To him there was no such thing as a friendly Indian. Even those reared in the missions, Cabello said, would revert to original type. Those who received presents and were befriended by the Spanish would be friendly in proportion to the gifts and other advantages enjoyed by the recipients. He favored bringing the Indians under military subjection, but he faced the same problem the fabled mice did in their solution of belling the cat. A great, applauded idea, but who's for putting the bell on?

In November, 1786, Cabello was made *teniente de Rey de Havana.* Except for the warring Indians, his administration might have been one of the most peaceful and routine.

RAFAEL MARTINEZ PACHECO
(1787-1790)

Rafael Martinez Pacheco was a political opportunist, mysterious and controversial, an apparent paradox. Most of the record is based on what he, or his enemies, said. Thus truth about him is elusive. He may have obtained the governorship by default (Bonavia Bernardo did not serve after being appointed because he was needed elsewhere) and his own indirect recommendation. He had the peculiar knack for effectively recommending himself.

In 1759 Pacheco petitioned the viceroy for a post in Texas. In listing his experience, he said he had helped Diego Parilla move the presidio of San Francisco Xavier from the San Marcos to the San Saba River in 1757, had recruited families to settle San Saba, and had served as conductor of supplies and horses for San Antonio. On November 23, 1763, he was appointed commandant of San Agustin. We have already seen how he was instrumental, with the involvement of governor-to-be Oconor, in effecting the downfall of Governor Martos.

In the fall of 1769 he was responsible for delivery of a group of shipwrecked families from the Gulf Coast to Natchitoches. He was made commandant of La Bahia in 1770, and aided Ripperda in campaigns against the warring Indians. Pacheco literally put the mission Indians on welfare; as long as they had plenty of beef and corn, he didn't have to bother with them.

Pacheco praised the missionaries and pictured them as underdogs standing up against the governors. They reciprocated by singing his praises. They said he brought a physician to San Agustin at his own expense to treat soldiers and Indians alike, that "aware of the effect of a good example he attended personally the evening services held in the mission and led the soldiers in prayer." "He has literally taken his food from his mouth that the sick may not want," a priest reported.

He wrote lengthy suggestions for improvement of government in Texas, saying that the chief trouble had been incompetent governors and presidio commanders. Most had limited experience in dealing with natives, were blinded by selfish interest, and had failed to cooperate with the missionaries. And many governors had engaged in illicit trade. This analysis proved him an astute observer and an effective phrase-maker.

About the next thing we hear of Pacheco is that he was governor of Texas. His appointment was dated February 21, 1787. There is little reliable evidence to measure the governor's administration against his stated standards. In one of his own accounts to the viceroy, we see him as a man of decisive, vigorous action: Cornered in a room in San Antonio by hostile Lipans, he finally succeeded in "unsheathing" his sword and transfixed the Lipan chief with such a mighty thrust that it inflicted a skin wound on an Indian beyond the chief. The room was

smeared with blood—on tables, chairs, walls, everything—
a picture of supreme heroism with the governor standing
stalwart with dripping sword in hand, master of his fate
as well as Texas'.

No question about it, the governor had a blessed talent
for any politician, that of never personally obscuring his
role as a hero and champion of threatened humanity. He
pleaded in behalf of the people that they be allowed to
brand cattle on the open range and that the cattle not be
declared property of the Crown. He got some minor concessions from the Crown and major applause from the people.

Pacheco was accused, in connection with Gil Ybarbo,
of smuggling. His administration seems to have faded out
into limbo. One historian said of this period that the office
of governor seems to have been eliminated and the province of Texas administered by a presidial captain. Pacheco
probably was ineffective for some time before the "viceroy" removed him October 18, 1790. Apparently opportunities in time ran out on him. His ending is as mysterious
and veiled as his beginning.

MANUEL MUNOZ
(1790-1799)

By the time Manuel Munoz became head of the province in 1790, the governorship, to a conspicuous extent,
either killed or corrupted its holders, or both. It had become increasingly difficult to keep a good man in the
governor's chair.

Reading Munoz' correspondence and reports, one would
think his administration was about as routine as anyone
could expect. That meant, in late eighteenth-century Texas,
that there was endless, petty, dull red tape: the documents
reveal in caricature a governor's role in provincial life. He

supervised trade among Indians and colonials and investi-
gated the age-old plague of illicit trade (it was still illegal to
trade with the French in Louisiana). He heard arguments
about how primary schoolteachers should be paid from the
government treasury, or should parish priests do the teach-
ing. He regulated Indian labor for construction and repair of
churches and priests' quarters, and ruled that such labor
required a permit from the commander general. He made
decisions about the purchase of "flour and wine . . . wax
candles and altar linens for celebration of the Holy Sacrifice." He made decisions on secularization of mission Indians, checked mission and presidio accounts, and had a
hand in locating mission and presidio sites.

Nothing monumental. But by 1796 the old man had
had as much as he wanted and more than he could endure.
He asked to be relieved because of failing health. He waited
for nearly a year before he received word that his request
had been granted and he had been promoted to colonel in
the royal armies. Antonio Cordero had been designated his
successor, but emergencies prevented his coming to Texas.
Then Jose Irigoyen arrived in New Spain with a blank commission for the first open governorship. He was tagged for
Texas but then became sick. Months lengthened into years,
and Munoz became an invalid, confined to bed.

The chief way out of the governorship in those days
was via death or scandal. Manuel Munoz went the way of
death on July 27, 1799.

JUAN BAUTISTA ELGUEZABAL
(1799-1805)

During Juan Bautista Elguezabal's administration, a
new problem loomed on the eastern frontier, the eternal
source of trouble of one kind or another for eighteenth-
century Texas governors. It was immigration, and it never

went away as long as there was a Spanish Texas. If
Elguezabal could have, in the fabled manner, stuck his
finger into the dike and plugged it, the history of the
Southwest doubtless would have been much different. But
he, like his predecessor, was tired, ill from hardships,
wavering in his decisions, and discouraged at wrestling with
a problem that nobody really knew how to solve. Also like
his predecessor, he was to wear out at his job unto death.

Spain ceded Louisiana back to France in 1800, and in
1803 France formally transferred Louisiana to the United
States. Many Latins in Louisiana petitioned Spain for "asy-
lum" in Texas, and the flattered Spaniards welcomed
them. Americans came too. Immigration policy was set
mainly from above Elguezabal, but with all his effort he
could not hold back even the trickle of American filibusters
he was ordered to stop. And the trickle became a flood of
land hunters with plows, driving stock and carrying rifles
in hand.

Elguezabal was born in 1741, became inspector of
presidios of Coahuila and Texas in 1795, and with the rank
of captain, made detailed inspections of La Bahia and
Rosario in 1797. He assisted Governor Martos during his
incapacitating illness, thus performing many duties of governor until he became governor *ad interim* on July 27,
1799.

In early 1799 he had issued a proclamation against introduction of merchandise from Louisiana. But by 1803
he said that it was futile to try to enforce it. The Alabama-
Coushatta and Choctaw Indians were brought into Texas
against his sanction and settled east of the Trinity River.
He thought all Indians fickle and insisted that they be kept
under supervision of experienced missionaries of mature
judgment. He died in office in San Antonio in October,
1805.

MANUEL ANTONIO CORDERO Y BUSTAMANTE
(1805-1808)

Manuel Antonio Cordero y Bustamante not only had an immigration problem in reverse to the old one (he, in time, wanted immigrants), but he had an outlaw empire as well on the eastern border. He became administrator of Texas in October, 1805, at the death of Elguezabal. He was, at the time, probably on his way to Nacogdoches at the head of troops to help defend the eastern frontier, for Spain and the United States (now the owner of Louisiana) were threatening war over the Louisiana boundary.

Cordero did not have to use his troops on the eastern border. War was averted by declaring the disputed territory between the Sabine and the Arroyo Hondo neutral in the fall of 1806. The arrangement prevented a war, but it caused no end of lesser troubles. Outlaws and the riffraff of the earth came pouring into this no-man's-land where no law existed. Naturally they spilled out at times into Texas, and they made travel extremely hazardous in crossing the zone. Efforts toward pursuing criminals into the strip or trying to police it brought warnings from the other side.

Cordero encouraged immigration as one of the most effective ways of building up a buffer against an aggressive and enterprising United States. This would serve his second plan, to build up a strong military force in Texas. Additional colonists could produce the additional supplies to support additional troops. He sent out invitations for immigrants, particularly craftsmen, and proved a prophet by theorizing that the Americans would be coming sooner or later, one way or another.

Cordero was an experienced frontier official. He was a lieutenant colonel in the Spanish army, and governor *ad interim* of Coahuila from March 26, 1797, until December,

1798, when he was appointed governor, a position he held with various interruptions until 1817. He was appointed successor to Governor Munoz but was unable to serve because he was leading a campaign against the Apaches. In early summer of 1805 he was appointed assistant governor of Texas because of the incapacitating illness of Elguezabal and the threat of war.

He encouraged friendly relations with the Indians as allies in defending the boundaries of Texas, and established the first hospital in Texas in 1806, mainly for soldiers. On April 24, 1807, Manuel Maria de Salcedo was appointed governor of Texas, arriving there in the summer of 1808. Cordero was directed to remain in the province to aid and instruct the new governor in his duties, which he did until 1810 when he returned to Coahuila, where he remained as governor until 1817.

Cordero was the frontier troubleshooter of this period. He was called from the governorship of Coahuila to administer Texas when it hung in the balance, to strengthen and militarily defend its borders, in general to set policy that would hold it secure for Spain, and in the end to prepare his successor to keep up the effort. It was all futile in the end, but he probably did as well as anyone available could have done. He was dealing with forces inevitably building up beyond any individual human control.

MANUEL MARIA DE SALCEDO
(1808-1813)

Manuel Maria de Salcedo was a fatal victim of the conditions and circumstances he pleaded and worked against. He possessed an unusual viewpoint of Texas, for he had lived across the border in Spanish Louisiana, where his father was governor, and had moved back to Spain with the family as late as 1803.

He was appointed governor of Texas on October 24, 1807, and took the oath of office that day in Cadiz. Arriving in Texas in the summer of 1808, he found the province a steam boiler under heavy pressure, agitating within by blind, blundering political intrigue and heated from the outside by restless American firebrands who thought Texas, and maybe all Mexico, should be a democracy like the United States. Actually, it seems, nobody knew precisely what he wanted, or how to go about getting what was needed.

Salcedo pleaded for more colonization as a safeguard against encroachment. He suggested immigration from Louisiana as more convenient and economical than from Spain. He pleaded for a port on the Gulf Coast to liberalize trade and rapidly develop the province, and urged development of resources to make the province self-sufficient. He failed, however, to convince his superiors of the dangers around them.

Salcedo tried little and big things on his own to the limit of his authority. He proposed driving the freebooters from the neutral zone. Impossible. With revolution brewing he proclaimed some strange, tedious laws—anything that might help. He proclaimed a curfew requiring all persons to halt when called on or risk being shot. Husbands were held accountable for wives out late. Shooting and shouting in San Antonio were prohibited as being bad for the nerves. Burning trash was forbidden because it might be used as signals for Indians. Dancing required a permit and was permitted only in a "house of good repute." Professional gambling and carrying of firearms were prohibited.

Without support from above, Salcedo was merely blowing against the wind. In 1810 revolution broke out in Mexico against centuries of callous, tyrannical government. Salcedo was overthrown by the Casas revolution in January, 1811, but was restored later that year as the result of a counterrevolution.

But the worst was yet to come from the outside. In 1811 Jose Bernardo Maximiliano Gutierrez de Lara, a blacksmith turned diplomat, went to Washington, D.C., seeking military support for the Mexican revolutionists. Failing there, he prevailed upon a young West Point graduate, Augustus William Magee, stationed at the United States Army post at Natchitoches, to lead an army of liberation into Texas. Magee recruited and mobilized his "Republican Army of the North" mainly in the neutral zone. It was probably as motley a collection as ever marched under one banner: desperadoes from the neutral zone, Creoles from the southern parishes, Indians from the wilderness, soldiers of fortune from everywhere, Americans from the four corners of the nation, Republican Mexicans from the native soil.

Salcedo and his Royalists fought a long retreat to San Antonio. His forces were finally defeated in the battle of Rosalis on March 19, 1813, and he and his staff surrendered as prisoners of war. Magee had died and Gutierrez was in charge. He was tyrannical and vengeful in the extreme. Members of the captured Royalist government, including Salcedo, were marched away, their throats cut, and their bodies left for the buzzards and coyotes to devour. Such Mexican cruelty and vengeance caused many Americans to desert, and the Republican Army of the North was later defeated. But it was too late for Salcedo.

The boiler had blown up from the effects of more patriotic fire than there were judgment and tolerance to control it. Salcedo was the victim of immature minds playing with the complexities of democracy.

JUAN BAUTISTA DE LAS CASAS
(1811)

Juan Bautista de las Casas had the golden opportunity to become the father of independence in Texas. Instead, he muffed his chance by becoming a despot.

When Hidalgo started a revolution in the interior of Mexico against despotism in 1810, many liberty lovers of Texas followed suit. On the night of January 21, 1811, opponents of the government effected a coup d'etat in San Antonio, with Casas as leader. At dawn the next morning, just as reveille was sounded, Casas and his supporters marched briskly to military headquarters and took over the troops, then placed Governor Manuel Salcedo under arrest.

About the only clear-cut issue in this revolution was that the present government was corrupt and the only means for getting a change was revolt. Outside of that, it was motivated by a strange muddle of ideas and issues. Independence was not generally sought; the Revolutionists, in the beginning, declared themselves for the king, a stand confusing to some of their brethren in the interior. But almost everybody was confused in those days.

Juan Bautista de las Casas was a retired army captain. His long hitch of soldiering had been primarily a monotonous routine of garrison duty, carrying out petty orders of his superiors while he rose slowly in the ranks. Nothing exciting or momentous had occurred to give him an opportunity to write his name on the pages of history. He still had dreams of conquest, of victory on the battlefield, of promotion and acclaim. But with retirement his military career was seemingly finished, and he was only a captain, just another name on the long military roster. Now with a revolution started, he had a feeling that his hour had come.

He knew little of what the commotion was about, but to him it had the rumble of a bandwagon upon which he might ride to glory.

Casas plunged into his administration with great energy. By nine o'clock of the first day of the revolution, he had freed the political prisoners in the guardhouse, and had ordered the arrest of all European-born Spaniards and the confiscation of their property. Before the day ended, he dispatched mounted troops to Nacogdoches and La Bahia to proclaim the new order there and to arrest the commanders and any others who refused to recognize him as governor.

Within two weeks the old government of Spain was overthrown and Texas was freed of the Spanish Royalists. Jose Mariano Jimenez, Hidalgo's colleague, sent Casas an appointment as governor. Then the revolution suffered defeats in Mexico, and dissension broke out among the leaders. By this time Casas was no argument for the cause. His lone-handed rule, lack of tact, severe treatment of opponents, and abuse of power turned fiery Revolutionists lukewarm and set Royalists to plotting his downfall. If this was liberty, then many former enthusiastic Revolutionists were not sure they wanted it.

Royalists and disappointed Revolutionists joined forces and started a revolution within a revolution. Most people did not understand the meaning of the words "liberty" and "democracy." They now considered any change better than what Casas was providing. Under Salcedo they at least had peace.

So on the night of March 1, another government for Texas was formed, and at dawn another leader, Juan Manuel Zambrano, took command of the troops at reveille and arrested the governor. A court martial in Monclova quickly found Casas guilty of treason, and on August 3, in compliance with his sentence, he was shot in the back as a traitor. His head was cut off, put in a box, and sent back to San Antonio. Here, where he had enjoyed the prestige and dignity of being first officer of the land, his skull was stuck up on a pole in the middle of the Military Plaza.

If Casas' head had not swollen so with power, his likeness someday might have been carved in marble instead of his head ending up bleaching in the sun on a pole before the eyes of his one-time followers. And freedom for Texas might have come sooner.

CRISTOBAL DOMINGUEZ
(1813-1814)

Cristobal Dominguez inherited the wreckage of the revolution, a revolution that produced nothing but hatred and division, that started out reasonably orderly and promising and ended in petty intrigues and bloody cruelty. It was not a big revolution as revolutions go, but the province was never the same afterwards—mistrust, instability, and property loss took a crippling toll.

With Salcedo killed, Jose Arredondo, commandant general of Eastern Interior Provinces, appointed Dominquez governor, subject to approval of the viceroy, sometime before August 26, 1813. Republicanism had been suppressed, American aid cut off, and royal authority restored; but the country was in shambles. Over a thousand terrified colonists and Indians had fled to the neutral zone in Louisiana, homes were abandoned, farms and herds left unattended, and the jails were bulging with prisoners. The dire prophecies of Salcedo had come true.

Dominguez was instructed to reorganize the province and restore order and confidence in the new regime. He set out to do the best he could. He tried to be firm with insurgent prisoners and their sympathizers, and warned against disloyalty. But his firmness had to be tempered for survival. Food and supplies were critically short. Workers were urgently needed. So he issued a proclamation of amnesty in October, 1813, granting a conditional pardon to those who had fled. Recognizing the need of the Indians' friendship, he made concessions to them such as reestablishing the trading post at Nacogdoches. He worked feverishly toward getting supplies from the interior—barely in time to avert panic.

Dominguez had extensive administrative experience. He was adjutant inspector of presidios for Coahuila and Texas when he was ordered to Nacogdoches on November 26, 1810, by Governor Salcedo. With the outbreak of the Casas revolution, he was arrested for his loyalty to the Spanish government, but he escaped and fled to Natchitoches. He returned to Nacogdoches after the overthrow of Casas and took over the duties of lieutenant governor until September 20, when he became inspector of presidios. He then held the rank of lieutenant colonel. Shortly after Dominguez became governor, Arredondo appointed him his second in command.

Dominguez doubtless did the best he could amid the chaos, which like the efforts of some other Texas governors was not enough. Also like numerous other governors, he wore out on the job and died in October, 1814, tired, discouraged, and old beyond his years.

BENITO ARMINAN, MARIANO VARELA, IGNACIO PEREZ, MANUEL PARDO
(1814-1817)

During the time of struggle for Mexican independence,

records are incomplete, and when available, often contradictory and otherwise confusing. We can do little more than list the chief executives during this chaotic period of transition.

Benito Arminan was appointed acting governor in 1814, following Dominguez, and served in that capacity until July 19, 1815, when he was permitted at his request to retire on account of failing health. He occupied himself mainly with the effort of securing basic necessities, including drugs, to keep his impoverished subjects alive. He kept an eye on marauding Indians and filibusters, but that was about all he could do.

Mariano Varela probably set a record for the shortest term. He served one week in July, 1815.

Lieutenant Colonel Ignacio Perez next served as *ad interim* governor, pending the arrival of Colonel Manuel Pardo. Perez is better known for his success as an Indian fighter, and for opposing the Long expedition and taking Long prisoners, than as governor.

Manuel Pardo took over as *ad interim* governor in early 1817 and served for a few weeks. He was born in Santander, Spain, in 1774, and fought in the European wars. After Texas, he served as governor of Coahuila and as a soldier in Mexico.

ANTONIO MARIA MARTINEZ
(1817-1822)

Antonio Maria Martinez had the sad duty of presiding over the collapse of the Spanish empire in Texas. He was the last governor of the Spanish regime in the province. Revolution had gnawed away at this remote corner of the empire until by 1821 it was all over and Mexico was an independent nation.

Martinez assumed the governorship in the spring of 1817. Nearly a decade of warfare had made Texas a "desert." Invaders came, fled when attacked, then came again. With his limited forces and supplies, Martinez could see little hope for defense. The treasury was empty, the Indians were out of control, foreigners could not be stopped on the border. For defense he had only about three hundred "pickets from the provinces" with little clothing, food, or military equipment. The governor reported that he doubted he could muster enough men to spike the common at San Antonio if necessary. Expeditions against invaders were possible only because men and supplies were sometimes furnished from the interior provinces.

Martinez was born in Andujar, province of Jaen, Spain. He enlisted in the military service July 7, 1785, and won the Cross of Northern Europe and the Cross of Germany on European battlefields. Texas was a pitiful climax for such a distinguished career. The old veteran could only appeal for supplies and men and watch helplessly as the empire he had fought for so valiantly crumbled about him.

In the summer of 1821 he was forced to issue orders requesting the oath of allegiance to Agustin de Iturbide, soon to become emperor of Mexico. Martinez was replaced in the summer of 1822, and moved back to Mexico to die a few months later, like many of his predecessors, discouraged and exhausted, in relative obscurity.

JOSE FELIX TRESPALACIOS
(1822-1823)

Jose Felix Trespalacios was a professional revolutionist who experienced its extreme hazard, the death sentence, and its ultimate glory, independence for his country along with personal recognition and reward. He was born in Coahuila, where he joined the militia in 1810. By 1814 he was sufficient revolutionist to be sentenced to death for conspiracy to provoke a rebellion in the interior provinces. His sentence was commuted to ten years in prison, but on the way to prison he escaped and again joined rebel forces.

In battle against the Royalists he was again captured, and again escaped. This time he went to New Orleans, and with the aid of local merchants organized an expedition to aid the independence movement. He joined forces with James Long, declared for the plan of Iguala (independence of Mexico), and was again imprisoned. He was released by the Iturbide government, and in late 1821, after independence, helped secure the release of Long and his followers.

He was appointed governor of Texas on August 17, 1822, and served until his resignation on April 7, 1823. Under his administration, the Stephen F. Austin colony was divided into the Colorado and Brazos districts.

He served as senator from Coahuila to the Mexican National Congress from 1831 to 1833, then went back to soldiering until his resignation, December 15, 1834. He died at Allende, Chihuahua, on August 4, 1835. No governor had lived more dangerously, or seen more of the worst and best of revolution and independence.

LUCIANO GARCIA
(1823)

Luciano Garcia was appointed *ad interim* governor of Texas on June 16, 1823, assumed duties of the office on July 8, and served in that capacity until October 12, 1823, at which time he became commandant general of the province.

The provinces of Texas and Coahuila were joined as

one state by decree of the Mexican Congress on May 5, 1824, with the provision that Texas was to be administered by a political chief. Garcia was appointed the political chief. He was friendly to the Austin colony, and completed its governing system by appointing the Baron de Bastrop as commissioner to extend land titles. He called the first elections in 1823 for the Texas representatives to the Constituent Congress of Mexico.

We are not entirely sure about administrators, titles, and dates during this period of sudden changes, but Garcia retired from the political scene in Texas sometime in 1826. And about this time he received a discharge as lieutenant colonel from the military, and devoted himself to stock raising.

After Garcia, Texas governmental affairs seem to have been handled, for a time, by political chief Antonio Saucedo. Garcia was the last chief executive of Texas before it and Coahuila were joined as one state.

3

Mexican Period

RAFAEL GONZALES
(1824-1826)

Rafael Gonzales was a native of Texas. Thus it seems ironic that he should serve as the first governor of Texas and Coahuila in remote Saltillo, Coahuila. But these were transition days when the new nation of Mexico was learning to govern itself, and among other things, transform provinces into states.

Gonzales served as governor of Coahuila and Texas from August 15, 1824, to March 15, 1826. The governor, now residing in the remote capital in Saltillo, was not so important and real to Texans. His orders came down through a chain of command. A political chief, appointed by and responsible to the governor, administered Texas; he resided at San Antonio, enforced the law, administered justice, and commanded the militia. Gonzales concerned himself mainly with securing more missionaries and having the missions secularized—trying to rebuild the state along the order of the old provincial concepts.

Texas was relatively quiet during his administration. The revolution was over. American settlers under Austin were quiet; immigrants could now come to Texas legally and in peace; and with stability, enemy Indians were less inclined to attack. The state was slowly recovering from the devastation of the revolution.

Gonzales was born in San Fernando de Bexar in 1789. He began his military career as a cadet in the presidial company of the nearby villa of Nuestra Senora de Loreto in 1806, and rose to the rank of captain in 1818. In July, 1821, he joined the independence movement and soon rose to lieutenant colonel.

In 1834 he was secretary of the *Comandancia* of Coahuila and Texas. The town of Gonzales, Texas, was named for him. Gonzales, the first governor of the Mexican state of Texas and Coahuila, died in 1857.

VICTOR BLANCO
(1826-1827)

Victor Blanco served a term as governor of the state of Coahuila and Texas from May 30, 1826, to January 27, 1827. His most notable action was the suppression of Hayden and Benjamin W. Edwards in the Fredonian Rebellion. He decreed the annulment of Hayden Edwards' contract by saying, ". . . it is not prudent to admit those who begin by dictating laws as sovereigns." Blanco, a citizen of Monclova, considered establishing a colony in Texas on the Trinity River and appointed Samuel May Williams as his agent to select a site, but the project never materialized.

On July 4, 1827, he was elected the first vice-governor under the constitution of Coahuila and Texas. He represented the state as a senator in the national legislature from 1833 to 1835 and was reelected in 1835. In this position he opposed Stephen F. Austin's request that Texas be separated from Coahuila. He engaged in war with Indians in Monclova in 1841, and later fought in the Mexican War.

According to Mexican historian Vito Alessio Robles, Jose Ignacio de Arizpe served a short term as governor preceding Blanco, from March 15 to May 30, 1826, and from January 27 to August 1, 1827, and that Blanco served as governor from August 17 to September 14, 1827. The date of Blanco's death is not known.

JOSE MARIA VIESCA
(1827-1831)

The tenure of Jose Maria Viesca reveals the unstable system of government as northern Mexico experimented with self-rule between national revolution and the revolt of Texas. According to Robles, Viesca's administration was chopped into three periods: August 1 to 17, 1827; September 14, 1827, to October 1, 1830; and January 5 to April 4, 1831. The period of October 1, 1830, to January 5, 1831, was filled by Licenciado Rafael Ecay Musquiz.

We know very little about Jose Maria Viesca. He was a brother of Agustin Viesca, who later served a shorter and more controversial term. Jose Maria, a native of Saltillo, represented his native Coahuila as a member of the deputation of the *Estado Interno de Orente* to the national Constitutional Convention of 1823-1824. He was a member of the legislature of Coahuila and Texas in 1824.

JOSE MARIA LETONA
(1831-1832)

If the policies and sympathetic attitude of Jose Maria Letona toward the Americans of Texas could have prevailed, the Texas Revolution might have been avoided, or at least put off. By the time of Letona's administration, authorities in Mexico City were becoming apprehensive about the flow of American immigrants into Texas, but the resulting attempt to stop the flow by a law of April 6, 1830, was too much too late. The law was intended to prohibit or limit effective immigration from the United States, and to prohibit bringing in slaves.

Letona's administration, from a Texas standpoint, concerned mainly the problems this law brought. He regarded it as unconstitutional, and with this view he sent Francisco Madero to Texas as land commissioner to survey and grant land titles. He also supported the land claims of the Cherokee Indians. The Law of 1830 is said to have been the same type of stimulus to the Texas Revolution that the Stamp Act was to the American Revolution.

Letona was caught in the middle between Mexico City and the American settlers. His overall administration dated from April 5, 1831, to September 18, 1832. By the time it was over, the Americans were restless and disturbed about their rights and future.

Letona, a resident of Saltillo, may have been the first lawyer governor of Texas. He participated in the Miguel Hidalgo y Costillo revolution under General Mariano Jimenez, and at one time served as his legal advisor. In 1821 he was a member of the provisional governing junta at Saltillo, which declared for independence through the *Plan de Iguala*.

He died, apparently in office, at Saltillo on September 18, 1832. His influence was sorely missed in the effort to hold Texas in the Mexican Republic.

JUAN MARTIN VERAMENDI
(1832-1833)

Juan Martin Veramendi had numerous personal ties with the Americans of Texas. These ties and resultant friendships bought some valuable time to enable the Americans to get settled and strengthen their position. In many ways he thought like the Americans. Texas was his native sod; he was born in San Antonio. He met Stephen F. Austin as early as June, 1821, and accompanied him to Bexar. He petitioned for a land grant under the colonization law of March 23, 1825, in the American fashion and received eleven leagues.

Veramendi married Josefa Navarro on December 17, 1778. They had seven children. His daughter, Ursula Maria, married James Bowie in the spring of 1831. He and Bowie formed a partnership in a cotton mill in Saltillo, and Veramendi divided his time between Texas and Coahuila.

In 1822-23 he was collector of foreign revenue in Bexar. Veramendi was the first *alcalde* of Bexar in 1824, and was elected vice-governor of Coahuila and Texas in 1830. As vice-governor he assumed the governorship on the death of Letona in 1832 and served until 1833, when he died of cholera.

JUAN JOSE ELGUEZABAL
(1834-1835)

The Texans had reason to expect better of Juan Jose Elguezabal than they received. He was a native Texan, and his father, Juan Bautista, was governor of Texas before him at the turn of the century. With this parental example, and having lived his life in the area, his background should have been as suitable for the governorship as any that could be found. But like his father, he faced problems too new to comprehend or solve.

Juan Jose was appointed governor in the summer of 1834 during a dispute that threatened civil war in Coahuila—a three-cornered ruckus among the state of Coahuila and the towns of Saltillo and Monclova. The details are too petty and silly to clog history with, but the quarrel rendered Elguezabal's administration ineffective as far as Texans were concerned.

He illustrates the dilemma of most Mexican governing officials of that period. He had neither example nor imagination to guide him. Whereas the English colonies had practice in self-rule under England, Mexico had known nothing but tyranny when independence came. Mexico was to flounder for decades before it could learn self-rule the long, hard way. This waste of time and blood illustrates that tolerance is one of man's most difficult and costly lessons to learn, that the use of gunpowder comes easier than reason.

Father Elguezabal's problem had been the effort to stop the immigrants. Now that they had come and settled anyway, the son had the opportunity to help provide a government they could live under and thus strengthen Mexico. Instead, he dissipated what energies and talent he had in petty details and squabbles.

While the political storm blew under gathering war clouds, Texas flapped like a barn door on loose hinges in the wind, ready to blow away at any gust, and the governor concerned himself with such matters as what was "urgently needed to re-establish peace in the colonies of Texas was a priest for the Department of the Brazos . . . a curate of good morals who does not meddle in politics," and worried over the circumstance that the matter should be "attended to as soon as possible because the marriages contracted during the last two or three years had not been legalized" and that "such a condition produced serious ills for society."

In spite of such social and legal shortcomings, the Anglo-Americans in Texas were getting along peacefully enough among themselves. They were Protestants, and marriages made legal by a priest who, to them, charged exorbitant prices in a money-scarce country had little to offer over their own private arrangements. What they needed most was political and economic stability. They looked on in disappointment and disgust at Mexican governing efforts and strengthened their conviction that they could rule themselves better by themselves, and might eventually have to do so.

Juan Elguezabal was born in San Antonio in 1781. His mother's maiden name was Maria Gertrudis Ximenes. He joined the army in Coahuila, became a captain and commandant of the Rio Grande, and like his father, adjutant inspector of presidios of Coahuila and Texas. He served as governor until the spring of 1835.

He rejoined the army under General Martin Perfecto de Cos, who established headquarters at San Antonio with the declared intentions of expelling all American settlers who had come to Texas since 1830 and arresting all Texas Patriots known to be odious to Santa Anna. This had all started because the Texans at Anahuac had protested the paying of duties. The Texans resisted and laid siege to San Antonio until Cos and his men, including Elguezabal, surrendered on December 10, 1835.

Elguezabal died in Matamoros in 1840. He had tried to rule the Texans as governor and then tried to defeat them as a soldier. He failed ludicrously at both.

AGUSTIN VIESCA
(1835)

Agustin Viesca made an effort to favor the Texans, but was from start to finish frustrated by numerous factions. The conflict was too far along, and the political situation too unstable, for him ever to govern effectively.

He was elected governor September 9, 1834, but the election remained in dispute until he took office about April 15, 1835. In the meantime, it appears two men served short terms as governor—Jose Maria Cantu and Marcial Borrego. As if the conflict between Texas and Mexico were not enough, Viesca was caught in a fight at home between the towns of Saltillo and Monclova over location of the capital. He assembled the militia to quell a revolt in Saltillo, but was ordered to disband by General Cos, who supported the clans of Saltillo. The legislature authorized him to move the government to any site he cared to select. He set out with the archives to San Antonio and urged the Texans to rise against the antirepublican movement.

He was ordered not to cross into Texas. He attempted, with some Texas-Americans, to escape into Texas, but was captured and sent as a prisoner to Monterrey. He escaped, and in November, 1835, arrived at Goliad. He expected to be recognized as governor, but the popular sentiment was strong against Mexico. He was well received by Austin and Texans in general, but no Texan wanted a governor elected under the Mexican constitution. The Texans preferred independence, and Viesca was not acknowledged as governor.

RAMON MUSQUIZ
(1835)

Ramon Musquiz deserves attention more for what he did for Texas before he became governor than afterward. His tenure as governor is a minor point for the record, for as a supporter of Santa Anna, he was from the Texas patriot point of view an enemy. But governing authority during this period was in a state of flux—often conflicting, overlapping, and indefinite.

Musquiz was vice-governor during Viesca's attempt at governing, and some historians regard him as constitutionally succeeding the governorship at the time Viesca became ineffective as governor—whenever that was. The chain of civil command in Texas frays out into limbo in 1835. After Agustin Viesca, it appears that one Miguel Falcon ruled for about a month, then Bartolome de Cardenas for three days in August, 1835, and then Santa Anna invested General Cos with both civil and military power.

Musquiz was a resident of San Antonio and operated mercantile businesses in Texas and Coahuila. In 1827 he was made political chief of Bexar, and in this position exercised great responsibility in administering the colonization laws for the early settlers. He was twice political chief of Texas and supported the settlers in many ways, once leading the San Antonio Board of Health in a preventive health campaign. He declared in favor of Santa Anna in 1832, participated in the settlement following the capture of San Antonio by the settlers in December, 1835, and was at the fall of the Alamo under orders of Santa Anna. After the revolution Musquiz returned to his native San Antonio to live.

4

Period of the Republic

HENRY SMITH
(1835-1836)

On November 3, 1835, a group of Texans met at San Felipe de Austin and set up a government of sorts—a ramshackle administrative machine called the Consultation, with built-in, unthought-out mechanisms sure to blow up even with a moderate engineer at its controls, which its first governor, Henry Smith, was anything but.

The "government" was basically a clearinghouse for revolutionary activities. It consisted mainly of an "advisory council" little inclined to limit itself to advising, and a governor who styled himself "Supreme Executive of the Free and Sovereign State of Texas" and was described as "every inch a king and would have been one if he could have been." Soon the governor and the advisory council were quarreling over their powers. The governor was an eloquent man even at slander and without the least inclination toward diplomacy. He referred to some councilors as rascals and "wolves out of the fold," and in time notified them that if they did not retract their errors, he would cease all intercourse with them by the next day. The council responded by promptly impeaching him.

Powers were not clearly defined. The council did not impeach after all. The governor did not quit either slandering or governing. The Alamo fell. But Sam Houston somehow managed to keep the army together in spite of the "government." The people were watching Houston more than the government and regarded him as the real savior of the country, if indeed it had one.

With all his faults, Smith helped to crystalize the spirit of independence. He pleaded for harmony, though he didn't know how to promote it himself. He wrote: "Nothing can save us but unanimity. . . . concentration and a bold, heroic movement of all our powers. . . . Texas expects every man to do his duty." With the declaration of independence and the election of 1836, the government was restructured out from under Smith. But he continued to serve, as secretary of the treasury during Houston's first administration and later in the House of Representatives of the republic, where he took a strong stand against financial inflation.

Smith was born in Kentucky on May 20, 1788, son of James and Magdalen Smith. He settled in what is now Brazoria County about 1827. He was severely wounded in the head in the battle of Velasco, was *alcalde* of the jurisdiction of Brazoria, delegate to the Convention of 1833, and in 1834 political chief of the department of the Brazos. He was from first to last a leader of the independence party. He married three sisters in succession, Harriet, Elizabeth, and Sarah Gillett, and was the father of nine children.

The spirit of indomitable adventure was strong in Smith to the last. He went to California in the Gold Rush of 1849 and died in a rugged mountain mining camp in Los Angeles County on March 4, 1851. Daring, possessed of more energy and dreams than patience and judgment, he never found either political stability or gold.

DAVID GOUVERNEUR BURNET
(1836)

The presidents of Texas were all dreamers. Perhaps it took visionaries with recklessness in their blood to brave the hazards of launching a nation born of war and molded under the shadow of it. Like most ambitious and speculative men who have striven for the peaks, these presidents spent time in the valley of despair, inactivity, or failure.

David Gouverneur Burnet appeared a born loser, but as with the other presidents, Texas was the supreme challenge of his life and brought a surge of his best, but not perfection, from him.

He lost his parents at an early age. He lost his first job because the firm he worked for went bankrupt. Worse still, he lost his inheritance of fourteen hundred dollars. He lost in his first military effort under Francisco de Miranda to free Venezuela from Spain in 1806, and barely escaped with his life. He went back with Miranda in 1808 and failed again. He went into business in Natchitoches, Louisiana, in 1813. Not only did the business fail, but he developed tuberculosis while working at it. Sick and depressed, he rode west into the wilderness and fell off his horse into the hands of the Comanches. Fortunately, the Indians nursed him back to health in a couple of years. He studied and practiced law in Ohio but his practice failed, and in 1826 he decided to make his home in Texas. He secured from the Mexican·government an impresario contract to settle three hundred families on a tract of land near Nacogdoches, but the enterprise was beyond his means.

The Convention of 1836 elected Burnet president *ad interim* March 16. His administration was trouble, hardship, and desperation from start to finish. His capitol was wherever he dropped his saddlebags. No money existed to operate the government or to support the disorganized army. He was too conservative to please the influx of soldier-adventurers, many of whom disliked the peace terms made with Santa Anna. A military clique tried to arrest him, but he stubbornly refused to resign. His courage may have saved Texas from military rule, which would likely have ruined the young nation's chance of recognition by other governments.

As soon as some measure of order was established, Burnet called an election, which made Sam Houston president. Burnet resigned October 22, 1836. He served as vice-president under Mirabeau B. Lamar until Lamar left office late in 1841 on a leave of absence because of illness and desperation.

After his term ended, Burnet went back to his farm, cultivated it with his own hands, and struggled unsuccessfully against poverty. Then came more losses. He lost in a campaign against Sam Houston for president, he lost all his children except one, and his wife died in 1858, leaving him disconsolate. He opposed secession, but his only son died in battle in the Civil War. He was elected to the United States Senate in 1866, but lost in the end because Texas was considered an unreconstructed state, so he was not allowed to serve. During his last years he was poverty-stricken and too feeble to work. He lived with friends.

On the successful side, Burnet was active in the movement for Texas independence, in the establishment of the new government, and in numerous official capacities. On the adventurous side, he is said to have given the command to fire the first shot for South American independence, for he was commander of the launch that led the attack under Miranda to free Venezuela.

Burnet was born at Newark, New Jersey, on April 4, 1788, son of William and Gertrude (Gouverneur) Burnet. He died December 5, 1870.

Burnet was an adventurer of the highest order, a man

David Gouverneur Burnet
1836

Sam Houston
1836-1838
1841-1844
1859-1861

of ideas but often unable to bring them to fruition because of temperament and lack of administrative ability, a man extremely sensitive to criticism, high-tempered, and inclined to argue when silence would have better served his purpose. Life gave and took from him in harsh measures.

SAM HOUSTON
(1836-1838, 1841-1844, 1859-1861)

Excitement, mystery, and romance followed Sam Houston like a shadow. He was famous before he came to Texas, which was the turbulent, dangerous, action-packed stage for his long, almost unbelievable finale. More has been written about Sam Houston than any other chief executive of Texas, most of it controversial. He did many things in many capacities.

Houston was born in Rockbridge County, Virginia, son of Samuel and Elizabeth (Paxton) Houston, on March 2, 1793. He moved to Maryville, Tennessee, while a boy, attended a few terms of school, worked in a store for a while, and not liking menial work, left civilization to live with the Cherokees for almost three years.

In 1813 he volunteered for service in the war with England. Later he fought against the Creeks and received wounds from which he never fully recovered. He resigned from the army in the spring of 1818, studied law for a short time, and in October of that same year was elected district attorney of the Nashville district. He had a fantastic record as a soldier, an enduring fascination for the military, and a natural talent for it that could not be hidden under the traditional bushel. So it is not surprising that he was appointed adjutant general of Tennessee, and in 1821 was elected major general.

His imposing figure, magnetic personality, and recognized capacity for leadership made him a natural in another field—politics. It was impossible for anyone to ignore Sam Houston, who may have been the most sensational dresser in America. His dress at one political meeting is considered characteristic: "bell-crowned, black beaver hat, standing collar . . . ruffled shirt, black satin vest and shining black trousers." In place of a coat, his broad shoulders were loosely draped with a "gorgeous" Indian hunting shirt, encircled by a beaded red sash with a polished metal clasp. "His socks were lavishly embroidered and his pumps set off by silver buckles." In Washington, as ambassador for the Indians, for every occasion he wore a new blanket with metal ornaments on his buckskin coat, tinkling pleasantly as he walked.

He also may have been the best mixer of his time. There was no need for Sam Houston to call. People of all types irresistibly flocked to him. No wonder he was elected to Congress without opposition in 1823, and easily reelected in 1825. In 1827 he was easily elected governor of Tennessee.

Then, in January, 1829, an eighteen-year-old girl named Eliza Allen changed the course of American history by marrying Houston. Before spring was well under way, Mrs. Houston returned to her parents. Houston resigned the governorship of Tennessee and returned to his Cherokee friends. He took an Indian wife named Tiana Rogers, and for the next six years he operated a trading post, used his influence to prevent trouble between the Indian tribes and settlers, and made periodic trips to Washington as ambassador for the Indians.

When talk of Texas independence spread, Houston rode into Texas and people congregated around him wherever he went. He served as a delegate to the Consultation, and was elected major general of the Texas Army on November 12, 1835. He signed the declaration of independence and a few days later was elected commander in chief of the Texas Army.

On March 11 at Gonzales, Houston took command of the little army of about four hundred men (statistics of this campaign vary). Two days later he received news of the fall of the Alamo. Houston could see no strategy except to retreat toward the Sabine. There was wide criticism, because security required cautious Texans to flee with the army. No one knew what was in Houston's mind, what he would or could do, where or when.

He made his stand at San Jacinto on April 21, 1836, and won one of the most extraordinary, sensational victories of all history. In a surprise attack lasting about fifteen minutes, he destroyed the Mexican forces that had chased him across Texas—630 killed, 208 wounded, 730 prisoners. Texas casualties were reported as six killed and twenty-four wounded. Houston, severely wounded in the ankle, went to New Orleans for surgery. By October he was sufficiently recovered to take the oath of office as president of Texas.

Houston could not by law succeed himself. Between his first and second term as president, which began late in 1841, he married twenty-year-old Margaret Lea of Alabama in May, 1840. As president he cut government expenses and reversed Lamar's antagonistic policies toward the Indians.

In 1846 Houston was elected to the United States Senate, where he served for nearly fourteen years. He was inaugurated governor of Texas in December, 1859. When Texas seceded from the Union in 1861, he refused to take the oath of allegiance to the Confederacy, and the Secession Convention declared the office of governor vacant. For the second time in his life, he walked away from the governorship to the solitude of the country, to be called ugly names by people who had once stood up and cheered loudly for him. There was another valley for Houston to walk through: his son was soon to be wounded and imprisoned as a Confederate in this war he abhorred. Houston's health began to fail.

But there was still magic in the Houston name. He was widely solicited to run in the election of August, 1863, for governor, but he formally declined on grounds of uncertain health. He died July 26, 1863, on his farm near Huntsville, survived by his wife and eight children.

The old wanderer was finally stilled. He had supped deeply from the bowl of life, the sweet and the bitter of it. He had dreamed magnificent dreams, and he had wrought some of them into glory.

MIRABEAU BUONAPARTE LAMAR
(1838-1841)

Mirabeau Buonaparte Lamar was Sir Galahad, Young Lochinvar, and King Arthur all in one stocky package. Only an ambitious, imaginative, distraught, at times slightly silly poet could have been perhaps the last knight— and president of Texas too.

Lamar rode into Texas from Georgia a few days before San Jacinto, long despondent over the death of his beautiful wife. He joined the retreating Texas Army as a private. On the eve of the battle of San Jacinto, Thomas Rusk and Walter P. Lane were surrounded by the enemy. It is said that Lamar rushed to the rescue, killed one lancer and put the others to flight, and thus rescued his comrades. Then Lamar calmly rode back toward his company, passing in full view of the Mexican lines. The enemy acknowledged their admiration by firing a volley in salute as he passed, and Lamar pompously reined in his horse and bowed in reply. This was Lamar in his glory. He was a true knight of old, charging full tilt across the plains of South Texas. The ancient steed, shining armor, and plumed helmet had merely given way to a Texas bronc, a baggy suit, and a flopped hat.

Recognizing his courage, the officers and men of the army insisted that he take command of the cavalry. He doubtless knew little strategy, and possibly only a few commands, but at San Jacinto he "swept forward on the right wing like an avenging fury . . . fought savagely, pursuing fugitive Mexicans, killing many, capturing few"— until Texas was won. Ten days later President Burnet appointed him secretary of war. Approximately a month after his enlistment in the Texas Army, he became a major general and its commander in chief. However, because he had fought in only one battle and a skirmish, the troops refused to accept him.

But heroes of his mettle could not be kept down in Texas. The people elected him vice-president in September, 1836, and he became president December 10, 1838. More visionary than practical, he favored sternness and force against the Indians rather than Sam Houston's conciliatory policy. His advocacy of public education earned him the title of "Father of Education," but little was actually accomplished. At his suggestion, Austin became the capital city. Always in debt himself, he ran the republic into debt. To draw attention from administrative problems, he opposed annexation, proposing a grandiose scheme that Texas should remain a republic, extended to the Pacific Ocean.

A charming, impulsive, generous dreamer, he was no match for rough-and-tumble politicians such as Sam Houston. He left office at the end of 1841 and spent his more peaceful and happy days on his plantation near Richmond, writing poetry and making gushy, patriotic speeches. He was now the Patrick Henry of Texas with a long, polished sword. He took time from the plantation to fight in the Mexican War, to serve as United States minister to Nicaragua and Costa Rica, and to marry Henrietta Maffitt of New Orleans in 1851.

He had been many things to many people since his birth on August 16, 1798, near Louisville, Georgia, a state where he had been a storekeeper, publisher, editor, state senator, secretary to the governor, and where he had married the beautiful Tabitha Jordan, whose early death drove him to despondence and away to Texas to forget. He died at his plantation on December 19, 1859.

ANSON JONES
(1844-1846)

Few men ever failed at so many things as Anson Jones. And few men ever brooded so much over failures. He was painfully shy and timid—highly ambitious but possibly the least aggressive politician who ever held high office in Texas. He obviously expected his talents to be adequately recognized, not realizing that for maximum public effect they needed to be demonstrated and repeatedly advertised—a serious oversight for any politician. When the war came, he served as surgeon and judge advocate, but insisted on retaining his rank as private.

He was a man of varying moods. Though generally pictured as a meek, timid individual without sufficient spunk for the rough-and-tumble politics of raw Texas, he pretty well covered the ground he stood on when the chips were down. Jones might "bow and scrape" and give up easily at times, but pushing him around was something else. When he returned from the war and found a prominent Texan using his office and refusing to relinquish it, he accepted a

Mirabeau Buonaparte Lamar
1838-1841

Anson Jones
1844-1846

challenge to a duel with him specifying "pistols at ten steps."

He served in the Second Congress. Then President Sam Houston appointed him minister to the United States in June, 1838. He managed foreign affairs until Texas joined the Union, thus gaining the title "Architect of Annexation." He was secretary of state during Houston's second administration and guided Texas through a series of crises.

Jones ran for president in 1844 in probably that state's oddest gubernatorial campaign. He did not make a single speech, saying, "it is against my principles, feelings and practices to go about electioneering. . . . The Presidency. . . is an office neither to be sought nor declined." Annexation was the burning issue, but he said a "discreet policy requires that I should keep silent." He was elected.

Being president in those formative days could not have been easy for a man even with steel for nerves. Jones was burned in effigy, and threats were made to overthrow his government. But he weathered the storms, and at the ceremonies setting up the government as a state on February 16, 1846, he declared that the Republic of Texas was no more, then retired to his plantation. He had married Mrs. Mary (Smith) McCrory in May, 1840.

He hoped to be chosen to the United States Senate, but Houston and Thomas J. Rusk were chosen. For twelve years he brooded over this neglect, though he accumulated a sizable estate during the time. In 1857 he believed his time had come and that the legislature would elect him as senator, but to the last he considered it proper to be asked rather than to ask. He did not receive a single vote.

Jones served Texas in some capacities of statesmanship that no one else was capable of, but he was so sensitive to criticism and slight that he suffered horribly from them, even to the unbearable point. On January 9, 1858, in Houston, he took his own life.

James Pinckney Henderson
1846-1847

5

State Period

JAMES PINCKNEY HENDERSON
(1846-1847)

It is probable that James Pinckney Henderson, the first governor of the state of Texas, did more for Texas outside its boundaries than within.

He came to Texas June 3, 1836, with a group of followers to join the revolution, but was too late for San Jacinto. David Gouverneur Burnet promptly commissioned him a brigadier general to recruit troops in the United States for the Army of the Republic. He organized a company in North Carolina and reputedly sent it to Texas at his own expense.

Henderson was appointed the Texas minister to England and France in 1837 with the result that both nations made trade agreements and in time recognized Texas' independence. In Washington he was probably more effective than any other man in ultimately influencing the United States to annex Texas. Even as governor, he left the state to serve its interest. When the Mexican War broke out, he secured permission from the legislature to lead Texans in battle in person rather than from the statehouse. He commanded the Second Texas Regiment at the

battle of Monterrey, and sat on the commission to nego-
tiate the surrender of the city. The United States Congress
presented him a sword for his gallantry, and appointed him
major general in the United States Army. Lieutenant Governor Albert Clenton Horton served as acting governor
from May 19, 1846, to July 1, 1847, while Henderson was
on leave of absence.

Henderson, son of Lawson and Elizabeth Henderson,
was born in Lincolnton, North Carolina, on March 31,
1808, attended Lincoln Academy and the University of
North Carolina, was admitted to the bar in 1829, and was
aide-de-camp and major in the North Carolina military at
the age of twenty-two and later colonel of a regiment. He
moved to Canton, Mississippi, in 1835. He married Phila-
delphia-born and Paris-educated Frances Cox in London in
1839.

He was a polished, formally educated man, described
as gentle as a lamb in peace and bold as a lion in face of
danger. He was of the stuff needed by the Texans, now
cocky over whipping the Mexicans, then bewildered and
embarrassed that the United States did not want them. He
was always the suave, confident, patient public relations
man who looked good and talked well for his fledgling
republic and state.

He served as attorney general and secretary of state for
the republic, then as governor of the state. He refused to
run for a second term as governor. He served in the United
States Senate from November 9, 1857, until his death on
June 4, 1858. He is buried in the State Cemetery in
Austin.

James Pinckney Henderson was a strong, guiding
force in the transition of Texas from a republic to a state,
both inside and outside its boundaries.

GEORGE T. WOOD
(1847-1849)

George T. Wood was a paradox. He was the representative type of aristocratic antebellum Southern gentleman planter and slave owner, yet he was careless about his personal appearance. It is said he never wore socks. Though an aristocrat, he apparently cared nothing for finery or the comforts of life. He made no effort to rebuild the burned-down executive mansion. He boarded at the old Bullock Hotel and left his family on the plantation. He rode a mule, and when on the road at night spread his blanket on the ground and used his saddle as a pillow. His wife apparently never came to Austin during his administration. He was a hardy outdoorsman of six feet and two hundred pounds, but he has been described by some as the poetic type.

Much of Wood's life was spent in politics. He was a member of the state assembly in his native Georgia in 1837-1838, member of the Texas House of Representatives in 1843, member of the Convention of 1845, member of the Texas Senate in 1846, and chairman of the first state Democratic convention. He served as governor from 1847 to 1849. He later ran in elections for governor and was defeated, it was said, because he was a Houston man.

He gained public recognition mainly as a military hero. At the age of nineteen he organized a company and fought with distinction in the Creek Indian War at Horseshoe Bend under Andrew Jackson. At the outbreak of the Mexican War he organized the Second Texas Mounted Volunteers and became a hero at the battle of Monterrey.

In his administration he was impulsive, fearless, outspoken. About the Indians, he said that they must "be pursued, hunted, run down and killed . . . Texas should offer a liberal bounty for their scalps." His record in the Creek

War and as a Texas Ranger left no question about what he meant. In addressing the state senate on the claim of Texas to ninety-eight thousand square miles of New Mexico, he said, "We will defend [every inch] to the last extremity, and if surrendered, it must be when Texas has no soldiers to defend it." Wood was so economical that he would have no house built for him and his family to live in. He repeatedly declared, "The public debt must be paid."

Born at Cuthbert, Georgia, on March 12, 1795, he married Mrs. Martha Evans Gindradt, a widow with three children, on September 18, 1837. In February, 1839, with his wife, four children, and thirty slaves, he moved to Texas and opened a large plantation on the Trinity River in present San Jacinto County.

Unconcern and neglect of person was his role even after death. He was buried on his plantation, and though a county was named for him, his grave remained unmarked for over half a century until the state erected one.

PETER HANSBOROUGH BELL
(1849-1853)

Peter Hansborough Bell, like his Anglo predecessors, belonged to that heroic age of Texas when chivalry and rugged individualism flourished. The Anglos had come to Texas without security of government or protection of armies. Perhaps nowhere were there ever so many opportunities for a man to show his mettle so quickly and prominently. The Texans found men among themselves who thought no worse of tomahawks than prickly pears and and would "charge hell with a bucket of water."

Peter Bell fit the heroic mold. Way off in Petersburg, Virginia, he heard of the struggle for independence, promptly closed his business, and headed for the fight. By the time he arrived, the war was almost over and he had no time to seek rank or position. He joined the army as a private just in time to fight at San Jacinto, but he fought so valiantly that Houston appointed him assistant adjutant general on his staff, and later inspector general January 30, 1839.

Bell joined the Texas Rangers and fought with the rank of major in the Somervell Expedition under Jack Hayes to punish Mexico for raids made in 1842. In 1845 he was captain of a Ranger troop assigned to "put the law in the Chaparral," a lawless area along the border. He accomplished his assignment and later resigned his Ranger commission to join the American army as a lieutenant colonel under General Taylor, and became a hero of the battle of Buena Vista. He served again as Ranger until near the time of his election as governor in 1849. He was re-elected in 1851.

Bell's administration was about as routine as could be expected for that time. The troublesome boundary dispute in which Texas claimed land to the west was settled in 1850 by the United States paying Texas ten million dollars for the land—a practical arrangement in view of the fact that Texas had much more land than money, and was deeply in debt.

Before the end of his second term in 1853, he resigned to fill a vacancy in the United States Congress caused by the death of David S. Kaufman, and remained in Congress until 1857. On March 3, 1857, in Washington, Bell married Mrs. Ella Reeves Eaton, daughter of a wealthy planter. The president served as host and master of ceremonies. Bell moved to her home at Littleton, North Carolina, and never returned to Texas.

Bell's beginning and ending were humble. Conflicting accounts of his birth permit us to say only that he was born in the early part of the nineteenth century, though we know he came of fighting stock of the American Revolution. The Civil War, in which he fought as a Confederate colonel, wiped out his fortune and left him penniless with only a small pension as a veteran of the Mexican War. He was a beaten man.

But in his heyday, he was magnificent in the eyes of the Texas voters. He was a blend of charming cavalier and rough-riding plainsman, skillful, graceful, and erect in the saddle, tall, slender, long black hair to the collar, a winsome smile for a greeting, but in a stern mood severe of expression. In civilian dress he was elegant and dignified, reserved and quiet. Polished and cultured gentleman though he was, he affected the practical garb of the Texas Ranger when on duty, two pistols at his side, a Bowie knife in his belt. He was a deadly shot with pistol and rifle.

In 1891 the Texas legislature voted him 1,280 acres of land and a pension of $150 a year so long as he lived. He died March 8, 1898, and was buried at Littleton. About a quarter of a century later the remains of Bell and his wife were moved to the State Cemetery in Austin, a fitting tribute to a man who had so often laid his life and talents on the line for Texas.

JAMES WILSON HENDERSON
(1853)

James Wilson Henderson was as willing and eager as any who came to fight for independence. He spent virtually all his active life in Texas in office or uniform, but he had only twenty-eight days at the top job of governor.

At the age of nineteen he left college to fight for independence, but arrived too late. He spent time in the United

George T. Wood
1847-1849

Peter Hansborough Bell
1849-1853

James Wilson Henderson
1853

Elisha Marshall Pease
1853-1857
1867-1869

States in the recruiting service, and worked as a land surveyor in Harris County, where he studied law and passed the bar. He participated in the Somervell Expedition, was elected to the House of Representatives of the republic in 1843 and 1844, and to the House of the first state legislature, where in 1847 he became speaker. In 1851 he became lieutenant governor, and when Bell resigned November 23, 1853, Henderson became governor until December 21.

He won reelection to the legislature in 1855, served as an officer in the Confederate army, was a delegate to the Constitutional Convention of 1866, a member of the Democratic State Convention of 1868, and vice-president of it the next year.

Born in Tennessee, he married Laura A. Hooker, and after her death, Saphira Elizabeth Price, and fathered five children. He died August 30, 1880, at the age of sixty-three.

Henderson did not serve at the forefront of leadership. He was a patient, do-what-is-needed man. Of such was the framework of Texas government in those days.

ELISHA MARSHALL PEASE
(1853-1857, 1867-1869)

Elisha Marshall Pease's public services spanned the plastic period between the Texas Revolution and the Civil War. He fought in the first skirmish of the revolution, and struggled at peacemaking during the agony of Reconstruction. He had the satisfaction of sponsoring the basic institutions required for the growth of a state, then the despair of seeing his early progress almost wrecked by division.

Development characterized Pease's administration. The

first free schools were established, appropriations made for creating a state university, institutions for the deaf, dumb, and insane founded, a new capitol and governor's mansion built, railroad construction pushed, state services advanced, taxes reduced, and the state debt almost eliminated.

His public services before the Civil War ran the gamut of jobs—secretary of the General Council of the provisional government, chief clerk in the navy, acting secretary of the treasury, comptroller of public accounts, district attorney of Brazora County, state representative and senator, and governor in 1853-1857.

Pease was a Unionist. After the Civil War he ran for governor on the Union ticket and lost, but he became provisional governor in 1867 by appointment of General Philip Sheridan. It was an agonizing job. In time he realized he could heal no wounds and still live with his backers. He resigned in 1869.

He became a leader in the Republican party in Texas, and opposed many of the harsh measures of Governor E. J. Davis during Reconstruction. In 1875 he became the collector of the port of Galveston. His last days were spent as a banker in Austin.

Pease was born January 3, 1812, at Enfield, Connecticut, son of Lorain and Sarah (Marshall) Pease, attended Westfield Academy in Westfield, Massachusetts, later clerked in a country store, and worked in the post office at Hartford, Connecticut. While in New Orleans in 1834, he heard stories of the promising land of Texas, and the next year, on his twenty-third birthday, he landed at Brazora with his wife. They settled at what is now Bastrop, where Pease began the study of law and was admitted to the bar in 1837.

Pease died August 26, 1883. He had seen the glory of the beginning, the anguish of the Civil War, and all between.

HARDIN R. RUNNELS
(1857-1859)

It is one of Texas' little political coincidences that the state's two most notable whittlers of wood should beat each other in back-to-back gubernatorial campaigns. Hardin R. "Little Dicky" Runnels defeated Sam Houston soundly to become governor in 1857, a historical feat within itself. Runnels whittled just about everywhere the notion struck him. Houston usually whittled out some wooden object in church while listening to sermons and then gave the trinket to some child after the service. Both men whittled white pine while thinking, but patterns of how they thought during those cutting exercises were obviously quite different.

Runnels took this stand: "The Southern states should look to themselves for the means of maintaining their future security." Houston said, "Texas will maintain the Constitution and stand by the Union." Houston stood for a conciliatory attitude toward the Indians and Mexico. Runnels tried to settle both problems with force.

A historian observed that there was more fighting in Texas in 1858 and 1859 than at any time save the revolution in 1836. During Runnels' administration, rifles flamed from the Red River to the Rio Grande. He decided the Federal troops were not aggressive enough against the Indians, so he strengthened the Rangers under Captain John S. "Rip" Ford and told him to do away with the Indians. But that was an impossible assignment.

Juan Cortina started a war along the Rio Grande to fight for the rights of Mexicans and raid United States livestock. Runnels was finally able to put Cortina on his own side of the border, but it caused a lot of bloodshed and a lot of bad feelings on both sides of that border.

Lynch law prevailed during this period. Law enforcement officers were too busy with Indians and outlaw Mexicans to protect the ranges adequately, and the stockmen often took matters into their own hands.

While war clouds boiled on the northern horizon and Runnels expressed his opinions on many national issues, the pot of violence continued to boil over in his own state. Sam Houston came back from the Senate to run against Runnels again in 1859. Still testy, cagey, full of fight, saying things no other man could and still live, he proclaimed that Runnels' policies just had not worked—and wouldn't. Representing himself as conciliatory and economical, Houston claimed that Runnels had been extravagant, favored reopening the African slave trade, and favored secession.

Certainly force had not worked successfully for Runnels. Of the Indian situation Houston said, in effect, that peace pipe smoke could have saved a lot of rifle and house-burning smoke. Possibly old Sam saw more clearly than anyone that force was not the best course whether for national or local issues, and he knew how to dramatize his point. Runnels lost.

Runnels, son of Hardin D. Runnels and brother of Mississippi Governor Hiram G., was born August 30, 1820, in Mississippi, moved to Bowie County about 1842 after his father's death, and established a cotton plantation. He was speaker of the Texas House of Representatives, and was elected lieutenant governor in 1855. He died December 25, 1875, and is buried in the State Cemetery at Austin.

Runnels had faced a difficult combination of problems— stubborn Indians fighting a last-ditch stand to hold their hunting grounds, embittered Mexican outlaws determined on vengeance and loot, division over states' rights, the popular appeal and oratory of the veteran Sam Houston smarting for revenge. It was a combination sufficient to bring the curtain down on *any* political career.

Hardin R. Runnels
1857-1859

Edward Clark
1861

Francis R. Lubbock
1861-1863

Pendleton Murrah
1863-1865

EDWARD CLARK
(1861)

In getting the job of governor, Edward Clark was the beneficiary of a fluke, and the victim of one in losing it. He ascended to the governorship by the oddest of circumstances. Governor Sam Houston, who refused to take the oath of allegiance to the Confederacy as required by the Secession Convention, was forced out of office. Clark, as lieutenant governor, thus took over the office. When Clark ran for a full term, Lady Luck again tipped the scales—this time against him. He lost by only 124 votes.

Clark was born April 1, 1815, in Georgia, and later moved to Montgomery, Alabama, where he studied law and passed the bar. Luck helped groom him by way of background to be a governor. His mother explained this at his inaugural ball on March 16, 1861: "It is natural to have governors in our family. This dress I now have on was worn at my father's inaugural ball in Georgia, later at my husband's [John Clark] inaugural ball in the same state, and now I am wearing it at my son's inaugural in Texas."

Clark had not only been associated with high politics, but he had been in it. He had sat as a member of the Convention of 1845 and as a member of both houses of the legislature. He was secretary of state under Governor Pease and was state commissioner of claims. He was elected lieutenant governor in 1859 on the Houston ticket, and he fought in the Mexican War. He was hero enough to fit the Texas mold.

His administration was perfunctory. The people's interest was mainly on the battlefield, where their men were, and Clark made a strenuous effort to produce and send arms and supplies to the front. He practiced what he preached about the war being his chief concern. As soon as he was defeated for governor, he raised a regiment and took the field until a rifle ball brought him down at the bloody battle of Pleasant Hill. He later continued in the war and was promoted to the rank of brigadier general.

Home from the war, he faced one of his low periods— an ex-governor, Confederate general, his old friends out of power, he feared vengence of radical Unionists and fled to Mexico. But soon he was back in Texas, engaged in various businesses at Marshall. But as always for him, outside of his profession there were still unpredictable ups and downs, so he resumed the more stable work of practicing law.

Clark was six feet tall, slim, of florid complexion, blue eyes, black hair and beard. He possessed a dignified manner and distinguished bearing, showed courtesy and consideration for everybody, and spoke with an eloquent flow of words, described as being of the "old regime—a type that has forever passed with that period."

Clark's first wife died shortly after their marriage, and he later married Martha Melissa Evans of Marshall. They had three boys and one girl. He died in Marshall on May 4, 1880, and was buried there. Life for Edward Clark was a series of good and bad breaks, Lady Luck a fickle mistress.

FRANCIS R. LUBBOCK
(1861-1863)

No governor so loved the Confederacy, had his administration so colored by it, and cherished its memory so dearly and long as Francis R. Lubbock. His administration was chiefly concerned with the war, securing raw supplies, manufacturing what he could, defending the frontiers against the Indians, and most of all recruiting men for the army.

He enforced rigid conscription and urged enlistment of

every able-bodied male between sixteen and sixty. He announced in February, 1863, that out of a population of about six hundred thousand, more than sixty thousand Texans had enlisted for the Confederacy. Nearly two thousand were in the Union army.

It was mainly because of disfavor of his rigid enforcement of conscription that he did not run for a second term, but he asked no more of anyone else than of himself. After leaving the governor's office, he promptly joined the Confederate army. He became a member of President Davis' staff, was captured with him after the war, and served a prison term.

Lubbock was born October 16, 1815, at Beaufort, South Carolina, son of Henry T. and Susan Ann (Saltus) Lubbock. He married Adele Baron in 1835, Mrs. Sarah (Black) Porter in 1883, and Lue Scott when he was eighty-seven. He engaged in numerous businesses off and on during most of his life, and served in various political capacities, including clerk of the House of Representatives in the Texas Republic, comptroller of the republic, district clerk of Harris County, lieutenant governor in 1857, governor in 1861-1863, tax collector of Galveston, state treasurer for five terms beginning in 1878, and member of the Board of Pardons. He spent his last years writing his memoirs, *Six Decades in Texas*.

Lubbock was a genial, exuberant, open, and joyous man, firm in his convictions, and not one to be tampered with. When Thomas W. Ward once struck him, he quickly drew his pistol and shot at him, barely missing. Lubbock was known for "various brands and styles of profanity" but never indulged in vulgarity. He was said not to be possessed of extraordinary ability, but always held public confidence.

For Francis Lubbock, the Confederacy never died—not in his memories, at least. He was one of the most touching and vivid reminders of the Lost Cause the capitol ever knew. On all important occasions there was sure to be seen somewhere in the crowd the bent, vivacious form of the little old man dressed in Confederate gray. And so it was until June 22, 1905, when the final bugle sounded for him.

PENDLETON MURRAH
(1863-1865)

Pendleton Murrah's administration was one of the state's saddest. The glory of war had faded into privation and misery. Texas was bled dry literally and figuratively. Dark clouds hung ominously in the east that might precipitate any disaster on the state. And the governor, a frail man, sensitive to frustration and defeat, was dying of tuberculosis.

Murrah's term was ushered in with cakes of cornbread served at a "state dinner," and his administration was cornbread-poor all the way. Seventy-four thousand Texans were dependents of soldiers and needed help that Murrah could not provide. Military and civil authorities clashed. Public funds were low, and there was but slight hard cash to pay taxes. Outlaws and Indians took advantage of undermanned law enforcement. Conflict over conscription continued to the last.

Born in South Carolina, probably in 1807, he was orphaned and never knew his parents. He moved to Alabama early in life and later to Marshall, Texas. He practiced law and was an accomplished orator. He married Susie Ellen Taylor, daughter of a wealthy landowner, but made a fortune of his own.

Murrah's political and military experience were slight for a Texas governor of this period. During the Know-Nothing excitement, he ran for Congress in 1855 on the

Democratic ticket and lost. He represented Harris County in the state legislature in 1857, and won the governorship in 1863. He had served in the quartermaster's department in East Texas but resigned because of his health.

Near the end of the war, rumors and threats of punishment circulated wildly. Southern governors were imprisoned. The following evaluation reveals a general feeling of the Texans: "The South is lost, hell's afloat, and the devil is to pay."

Murrah knew death was near for him. On hearing of the surrender of the Confederate armies in 1865, he turned the governorship over to Lieutenant Governor Fletcher S. Stockdale (who held it from June 11 to July 25), put on his old gray uniform, mounted his old war horse, and rode away to Mexico, to die later that year (probably August 4) if not in peace of mind, at least away from the clamor and hate and emotional turmoil of his war-torn homeland. He was buried in Monterrey, but his grave is lost in a foreign country. It was a sad time for a sensitive, noble man, as well as for Texas and a divided nation.

ANDREW J. HAMILTON
(1865-1866)

Andrew J. Hamilton was appointed to govern a defeated, disorganized, debt-ridden Texas on June 17, 1865, but it was July 25 before he arrived and took office. It is generally considered that he was as well qualified as anyone available, and proved as popular as could be expected under the circumstances. He had held public office in Texas, but like Sam Houston, opposed secession. As a Unionist he had barely escaped the state with his life and gone to Washington.

He did the best he could to restore civil government,

fill vacated offices, and govern under presecession law. His chief objective was to get Texas back into the Union as a full-fledged state as quickly as possible, but due to military authority he was more a figurehead than a governing official. He served for slightly over a year—to August 9, 1866, when James Webb Throckmorton, elected by the people, took over.

Hamilton had been attorney general of Texas, member of the House of Representatives, and member of Congress as an Independent, where he remained after other Southern members withdrew. In 1866, after his governorship, he received an appointment as associate justice of the Texas Supreme Court. He ran against E. J. Davis for governor on the Conservative ticket in 1869 and lost by less than a thousand votes.

Born January 28, 1815, in Huntsville, Alabama, Hamilton came to LaGrange, Texas, in 1846 and practiced law. He died in Austin on April 11, 1875. He had tried to bring unity to his divided Texas, but passions ran too deeply. Conditions had to get worse before they could get better.

JAMES WEBB THROCKMORTON
(1866-1867)

James Webb Throckmorton was the only doctor to serve as governor of the state of Texas. No governor ever had a sicker state for a patient, but he had little time to cure ills in his one year—or a little less—though he tried a lot of political physic.

He was elected governor in the summer of 1866 and served until midsummer, 1867, when General Philip Sheridan removed him as "an impediment to Reconstruction." The exact date of his leaving office is uncertain.

Andrew J. Hamilton
1865-1866

James Webb Throckmorton
1866-1867

Edmund Jackson Davis
1870-1874

Richard Coke
1874-1876

Throckmorton chided Union troops for lolling in comfortable quarters while frontiersmen, trying to protect their families, were dying in bloody battles against the Indians. He tried to make Texas a full-time partner with the Union, and helped promote building of the Texas and Pacific Railroad.

His politics did not stop with his ouster from the governor's office. He was elected to Congress and served intermittently until 1888. One of the first to propose some control over railroads, he ran for the Democratic gubernatorial nomination in 1878 and was defeated, and he had to withdraw from a gubernatorial race in 1890 because of his health.

He was born February 1, 1825, at Sparta, Tennessee, son of Dr. William E. and Elizabeth (Webb) Throckmorton. The family moved to Arkansas, then to Texas in 1841. He served in the Mexican War as a surgeon. He married Annie Rattan of Illinois in February, 1848. After 1859 he studied, then practiced, law. He served in the Texas legislature and was one of the famous seven to vote against secession, but he served in the Confederate army, though "knowing" it was a lost cause.

He died April 21, 1894—doctor, lawyer, soldier, statesman, good at them all.

EDMUND JACKSON DAVIS
(1870-1874)

Edmund Jackson Davis was probably regarded by many Texans second only to John A. Murrell as a villain. There was a strong parallel between him and the preaching bandit—Murrell hid in the pulpit, while Davis promoted his devilment from the governor's office. Both were intelligent and suave, and both may have been honest in their convictions that some people, even classes of them, needed to be done away with one way or another. Murrell operated on a wider scale, posing as a preacher while plotting the downfall of the South by means of a slave rebellion. Davis limited his operations to the downfall of the Confederates in Texas. And both men used just about every type of character to get their work done.

Both men apparently turned to bitterness and revenge because of defeats. Murrell, after a hard-fought trial, was branded and sent to prison. Davis, who suffered defeat as a candidate to the Secession Convention, later was caught in Mexico by a daring band of Texas Rangers and scheduled to be hanged, but he escaped the rope—to many Texans the most regrettable instance of carelessness in Texas history. This narrow escape from the rope no doubt further inflamed his hatred of Texans.

Davis, born in Saint Augustine, Florida, on October 2, 1827, came to Texas in 1838. His wife was Anne Britton. He practiced law, was a district attorney, then a judge until the Civil War.

He organized a regiment of cavalry, mainly Texas Unionists, and escaped to Mexico. He led the unsuccessful Union attack on Laredo in 1864, and was made a brigadier general after the battle of Mansfield. His war records reveal no brilliant exploits, probably in part because of the quality of men he surrounded himself with. His troops at disbandment were described as "the greatest aggregation of scoundrels and cut-throats that ever disgraced a uniform."

Davis beat former governor A. J. Hamilton for governor in 1869 by approximately eight hundred votes, in an election conducted by the Republicans and generally thought won by fraud and intimidation. He was an arrogant dictator for the next four years. Intimidation, inefficiency, extravagance, and corruption were the order of the day. Riots and terror resulted from actions of the state police, composed largely of blacks. By authority of the "Carpet-bag Constitution," he appointed more than eight thousand officials. He declared martial law at his pleasure, and required the counties occupied to pay for living expenses of the enforcing troops. He was the leader in the movement to divide Texas into three states, and nearly succeeded. One historian described his administration as "a carnival of crimes."

In the gubernatorial campaign of 1873, Richard Coke beat Davis by a large majority, but Davis refused to give up the office, fortified himself with Negro guards on the first floor of the capitol, and wired President Grant to send troop reinforcements to back him. Coke and his newly elected legislature maintained their position on the second floor. A local civil war appeared likely to start at the pull of a trigger during the dual governorship, until Grant refused to intervene. It is said that at this news and the capitulation of Davis, Mrs. Davis snatched the elegant portrait of President Grant from the wall, stomped it, and ground her sharp shoe heel through the eyes of it.

Davis ran on the Republican ticket against Oran Roberts in 1880 and was soundly defeated. He remained the leader of the Republicans until his death on February 7, 1883.

To use the parallel with John A. Murrell all the way is not fair to Davis. His is an intriguing, puzzling study of character: He was narrow and intense in his views, incapable, it is said, of seeing more than one side of any question, but he had nerve, to back his hatreds or anything else.

When he was waiting to be hanged, watching four of his comrades drop to inglorious death at the end of a rope, he calmly rolled a cigarette and leisurely inhaled it, blowing smoke with as much apparent relish as if at a banquet. His nonplussed captors gathered around to observe his

courage, a delay that gave Mexican authorities time to arrive and successfully demand his release on grounds of
neutrality laws.

A political enemy said that as a Republican, Davis was
"rank pizen" but was clean personally and socially. He said
of his business dealings with Davis, "His word was as good
as any Democrat in Texas"—one couldn't pay a man in
Texas a higher tribute in those days. But Davis' hatred,
bitterness, and narrowness were a yoke the people of
Texas had to bear when their burdens were already almost
beyond endurance.

RICHARD COKE
(1874-1876)

Richard Coke's inauguration in January, 1874, was the
dawn of a new era after a dark night. His administration
ended Radical rule and restored the government to the
people. He faced problems—Indian raids on the frontier,
Mexican forays, decisions about subsidies and routes for
railroads—but at last the governor was his own man, and
the people rejoiced at the new freedom.

Coke was born in Williamsburg, Virginia, on March 13,
1829, son of John and Eliza Coke. He graduated from
William and Mary College in 1849, passed the bar in 1850,
and practiced law at Waco. He married Mary Horne of
Waco in 1852, and four children were born to them.

He enlisted in the Confederate army as a private and
was discharged as a captain. He was a district judge, then
judge of the Texas Supreme Court until Sheridan removed
him as "an impediment to Reconstruction." Coke was
reelected governor in 1876, but resigned later to take a seat
in the United States Senate, where he served three terms.

He was an unpretentious man of large stature, with a

massive bald head, a heavy growth of beard, and a deep
voice that "roared like a bull when angry." An acquaintance related that he always carried a Bible in his pocket.

Coke died at Waco and was buried there in 1897. He
had seen law and order established in Texas, and the state
represented with respect and distinction in the United
States Senate.

RICHARD B. HUBBARD
(1876-1879)

Richard B. Hubbard was no ordinary man, and his administration was not ordinary. He was the biggest and
loudest governor Texas ever had; he weighed over four
hundred pounds, and it was said he could be heard for
miles. He used his extraordinary features to advantage,
cultivating his powerful, melodious voice until he gained
the sobriquets of Demosthenes of Texas and the Eagle
Orator. And he carried his bulk in such a way as to make
himself extremely impressive.

Hubbard was never elected or formally defeated in a
gubernatorial election, though he ran. He rose to governor
from lieutenant governor in December, 1876, when Coke
resigned to become senator. When he later ran for governor
against two other candidates, none received a majority. As
a result, one of the strangest devices ever conceived for
choosing a governor defeated him. A committee of thirty-
two, made up of friends of the candidates, were instructed
to meet and by vote choose their favorite. On the fourth
ballot the committee gave Oran M. Roberts a majority of
eighteen, so he became governor.

It might seem that Hubbard would have had one of the
most leisurely, trouble-free administrations of all time, for
the legislature did not meet during his entire administration

except to inaugurate his successor. But each era of history seems to have a way of producing its own peculiar brand of problem. Governor Coke had been able to initiate some stability out of Radicalism, but the Civil War had gotten many people into the practice of shooting their neighbors in a way that was considered proper and even honorable. By the time Hubbard came along as governor, a lot of the boys who had been trained to shoot their neighbors in organized fashion had grown up into business and professional men, now touchy about such things as property and reputations of one sort or another.

There has always been about as little stigma attached to shooting people in Texas as anywhere—with savage Indians, invading Mexicans, and outlaws of nearly every ilk stalking the land. So in this era when men got into disputes they often collected their friends and declared little ad-lib civil wars here and there just about all over the state. Such mini-wars were called feuds in Texas. Some lusty, especially talented marksmen such as Sam Bass, John Wesley Hardin, and Ben Thompson were rugged individualists who never bothered to get organized. They operated purely free-lance. Some of the most troublesome wars were the Horrell-Higgins and Taylor-Sutton feuds and the Mason County and Salt War of El Paso.

It might seem that the most practical thing for Governor Hubbard to have done would be to let the contestants dispose of themselves with their own lead, but he worried a great deal about what he called law and order. First he encouraged local authorities to maintain the peace, with the chief result of getting some prominent deputies buried. Seeing that the situations were more serious than he thought, he worked his Texas Rangers overtime. Actually, nothing very effective has ever been found to stop wars, little or big, so the "Terrible Seventies" more than anything else just wore out into the "Better Eighties."

Little that was new occurred in Hubbard's administration. The Farmers' Grange became a factor in politics, and primary elections began to take the place of ward meetings and precinct conventions.

Born in Walton County, Georgia, on November 1, 1832, son of Richard Bennett and Serena (Cartor) Hubbard, he graduated from Mercer College and Harvard Law School, and practiced law in Tyler, Texas. President Buchanan appointed him United States district attorney of the Western District of Texas in 1858. He later served in the state legislature, and during the Civil War commanded the Twenty-second Texas Regiment of cavalry as colonel. He served from 1885 to 1889 as United States minister to Japan. His *The United States in the Far East* was published in 1899.

He was married first to Eliza Hudson and later to Janie Roberts. He died July 12, 1901—an extraordinary man who had governed at the end of the extraordinary "Terrible Seventies."

ORAN M. ROBERTS
(1879-1883)

One can't read accounts of Oran Milo Roberts without their conjuring up a kaleidoscope of images: A man riding nonchalantly from a small farm into town on a fantail, spotted pony, in an incongruous Prince Albert coat, puffing a corncob pipe, to borrow "four bits" from a local bartender to send a telegram to the nominating convention to accept the nomination for governor of Texas. A chief justice of the state supreme court shucking off his black robe to don an army uniform of Confederate gray. A manly, stern governor weeping over the pleas of wives and mothers begging for pardons to save their men from the gallows, crying because he could not see according to the law why the terrible sentence should not be fulfilled. A firm, cautious, tender-hearted man telling schoolteachers and parents that school funds must be cut, telling veterans of the Texas Revolution that their pensions must be lowered, telling scared citizens that rewards for arrests of criminals must stop and some convicts have to be set free to save the cost of crowded prisons—all to save money to eliminate the public debt and put the government on a "pay as you go" basis. An indignant, hurt student of the law being told that Texas is going to hell because of his abuse of the pardoning laws, then storming back at them with "If Texas goes to hell under my rule it will go according to the law," because he always had to feel that what he did was strictly according to law. A great, sensitive scholar and writer leading an infantry charge, yelling orders, and flaying his sword in animated gestures, pointing directions amid the roar and smoke and blood in the thick of it. And finally a sharp-faced old man with black eyes that still sparkle, dressed as ever in a faded Prince Albert coat, puffing occasionally on an old corncob pipe as he bends over scattered notes, shuffling them into order to write a scholarly volume on the meaning and practice of the law.

Economy was the keynote of Roberts' administration. He paid off half a million dollars of the public debt, and left a cash balance of $300,000 in the treasury. He sponsored a unique law to obtain revenue by a tax on drinks sold in saloons, known as the "bell punch law." The number of drinks sold was to be registered by turning a crank and ringing a bell somewhat in the manner of train conductors keeping accounts of tickets punched. Provisions were made to sell three million acres of vacant land in the Panhandle to pay the cost of replacing the capitol destroyed in 1881, a capitol without public funds or taxes—that was Roberts to the core. Texas University was opened in 1883 during his administration.

Richard B. Hubbard
1876-1879

Oran M. Roberts
1879-1883

John Ireland
1883-1887

Lawrence Sullivan Ross
1887-1891

Roberts' accomplishments were so numerous that they can only be listed. He moved to Texas and opened a law practice in San Augustine in 1841. He became a district attorney, district judge, president of the Secession Convention, commander of a regiment of Texas infantry, chief justice of the Texas Supreme Court, member of the Constitutional Convention of 1866, member of the Texas legislature, United States senator (but was not allowed to serve), and head of a school of law at Gilmer.

He was nominated for governor in 1878 without solicitation or consent, and it is said that his entire campaign expenses consisted of thirty-five cents for a telegram accepting the nomination. He became professor of law at Texas University, where he was known as "Old Alcalda." He spent his last days writing a number of scholarly books on law and history. He was an organizer and first president of the Texas State Historical Association.

Roberts, son of Obe and Margaret (Ewing) Roberts, was born in Laurens District, South Carolina, on July 9, 1815, graduated from the University of Alabama, and served a term in the Alabama legislature. He married Frances W. Edwards in 1837, and they had seven children. In 1887 he married Mrs. Catherine E. Border.

Roberts died in Austin on May 19, 1898—a colorful, remarkable man who had done so many things well that no one, doubtless with the exception of Sam Houston, was better known in Texas.

JOHN IRELAND
(1883-1887)

John Ireland was so apprehensive and baffled by much of the new and changing times that many people called him "Oxcart John" because they thought he clung too cautiously to the old and familiar. He was an odd conservative in a period when progress and development were the talk of the masses. He was even an isolationist when expansion in economics and politics was coming into vogue. He said, "Our fathers were happier and freer and more prosperous with oxcarts and living in log cabins than their children in the days of steam and electricity." As an isolationist, he repeatedly warned against outside capital. He feared foreign immigration into Texas, and warned that the day would come when "the ignorant hordes of Europe and Asia will be elbowing our children into the sea."

Ireland's most vexing problem was the fence or "wire" cutters. He obviously shared Big Foot Wallace's observation, "The railroads and barbed wire have played hell with Texas." The free grass system resulted in the enclosure of large areas of land by cattle barons, often enveloping and shutting in smaller stockmen, excluding them from access to water and grazing land. This caused just what might be expected—organized, widespread cutting of fences of lawful owners as well as those of intruders. This headline exemplifies the extent of the devastation: "Five Hundred Miles of Wire Fences Cut in Coleman County." It took the governor, a special session of the legislature, and the Texas Rangers to stop the "war."

Then in 1885 and 1886 the Knights of Labor tangled with capital—something else new and big to Ireland. He went to the scenes of trouble and assured the strikers that the law would be enforced, law that in time was interpreted by some governors as too much on the side of capital. He faced the new problem head-on and arbitrated labor-capital disputes, a first for a Texas governor.

He had new little problems as well as big ones. Engineers told him that limestone for constructing the new capitol building would have to be imported from Indiana. As the final arbitrator in the matter, he declared, "I'll be damned if the capitol isn't going to be built of Texas material." And it was—of Texas granite. A newly recognized problem was the increasing bigness of government. He urged the legislature to set up bureaus, commissions, and committees to handle the growing complications of governing Texas.

Ireland was born January 21, 1827, near Millerstown, Kentucky, son of Patrick and Rachel (Newton) Ireland, of a family of six sisters and seven brothers. He was sheriff of his home county, started practicing law in Seguin, Texas, in 1853, and was the town's mayor, then a delegate to the Secession Convention, and later a colonel in the Confederate army. He served as a district judge, in the House and Senate of Texas, and as an associate justice of the Texas Supreme Court. Ireland ran twice unsuccessfully for the United States Senate. He was elected governor in 1882 and again in 1884. After leaving the governorship, he practiced law at Seguin until his death on March 15, 1896.

He had married Mrs. Matilda (Wicks) Faircloth in 1854, and after her death married Anna Maria Penn in 1857. He was the father of five children.

Ireland, with good common sense and a studious approach, adapted to current conditions and led his state through a troublesome period of change. And "Oxcart John" in time became an affectionate rather than a derisive nickname.

LAWRENCE SULLIVAN ROSS
(1887-1891)

With Lawrence "Sul" Ross, the age of "the Confederate Brigadier" passed. But to many he was the epitome of the lot—the most exciting, brave, chivalrous, and knightly of all.

He was one of the most courageous and effective Texas Rangers before and after the Civil War, killing some of the most noted and troublesome Indian warriors in hand-to-hand combat. He rescued the famous Cynthia Ann Parker, captured by the Comanches when a child and mother of the famous Quanah Parker. Few saw more combat in the Civil War—a hundred thirty-five military engagements. He was more characteristically Texas than the governors up to his time, for he was reared here, fought the Indians on the frontier as a boy and man, and was twice captured by them and held at their mercy.

He had a great stake in Texas, but he felt that the less he, or anybody else, ruled it, the better. "That government is best which governs least," he said. His administration was known as "the era of good feeling in Texas," with unusual peace, progress, and prosperity.

He sponsored laws prohibiting dealing in cotton futures, closed sale of public lands to corporations, and made a beginning in regulating railroads. He was the first to occupy offices in the new capitol building. He established Arbor Day, and sponsored funds to purchase the Henry Huddle gallery of portraits of all the chief executives of Texas.

Ross was born September 27, 1838, at Bentonsport, Iowa, son of Captain Shapley P. and Catherine (Fulkerson) Ross. He was brought to Texas in a prairie schooner as a baby. He graduated from Wesleyan University in Florence, Alabama, in 1859.

After the war he was a farmer, Texas Ranger, sheriff of McLennan County, state senator, governor from 1887 to 1891, then president of Texas Agricultural and Mechanical College until his death in Waco on January 3, 1898. He had married Elizabeth Tinsley in Waco in 1859. She and six children survived him.

If "Sul" Ross can truly be called the last of the Brigadiers, he was certainly one of the most sensational and useful of them all.

JAMES STEPHEN HOGG
(1891-1895)

No governor, up to his time, cast such a long shadow as James Stephen Hogg. He was all Texan, the first native son to become governor of the state. Orphaned at twelve, the family plantation sold to pay taxes, limited to scant formal education, Hogg knew the plight of the common man and became his most notable champion in Texas to that time. Hogg contended that the people should regulate the big corporations and money interests rather than be subject to those interests. His administration marked the transition from the older policies of the Civil War and Reconstruction days to newer economic issues, in time called "progressive."

As attorney general, Hogg, through suits or influencing legislation, got a fair start in his long fight against corporate interests. He instituted suits that in time returned over one and a half million acres of land to the state. He fought to enforce laws requiring railroads and land corporations to sell their holdings to settlers within a certain time. He broke up the Texas Traffic Association, which was formed by the roads to pool traffic, fix rates, and control competing lines, in violation of law. He forced wildcat insurance companies to quit the state, helped write the second state antitrust law in the nation, gradually compelled the railroads to enforce Texas law, and advocated establishment of the Railroad Commission. Hogg was elected governor on this platform in 1890.

Laws passed under his administration included establishment of the Railroad Commission, a law cutting down on watered stock, one forcing land corporations to sell off their holdings in fifteen years, and one checking further land grants to foreign corporations in an effort to get the land into the hands of the citizens. He also secured financial aid for a department of state archives.

Hogg was born near Rusk on March 24, 1851, son of Joseph Lewis and Lucanda (McMath) Hogg. His father, a brigadier general in the Civil War, died at the head of his command in 1862, and his mother died the following year. He improved his vocabulary by working in a newspaper office, in time operating his own newspapers in Longview and Quitman. He married Sallie Stinson in 1874, and was admitted to the bar the following year.

When he retired from the governorship in 1895, he declared he was in debt, but by his law practice and investments in city properties and oil lands, he accumulated a sizable fortune. He died March 3, 1906, of injuries received in a railroad accident. He had not succeeded in getting all his policies enacted into law, but his influence prevailed among the people and succeeding officials until, to a practical degree as he had envisioned it, corporate powers were brought under control.

Hogg was a giant of a man, possessed of a magnetic personality and unrivaled capacity in his time as a stump speaker. Because of his stand against privileged classes, he was called the "Great Commoner" and the "Great Reformer." It was said of him, "He always led, never followed," and "There was no power behind the Hogg throne."

CHARLES A. CULBERSON
(1895-1899)

Charles A. Culberson was known as "Our Christian Governor," a title he gained from his early stand against prizefighting. It was an easy and appropriate title to wear

James Stephen Hogg
1891-1895

Charles A. Culberson
1895-1899

Joseph Draper Sayers
1899-1903

at the turn of the century. He was one of Texas' most handsome governors; he dressed immaculately and was cultured and reserved in manner. After serving two terms as governor, from 1895 to 1899, he served twenty-four years in the United States Senate, and many think he would have been president of the United States but for his failing health (his last few years in the Senate were spent in a wheelchair).

When the Robert Fitzsimmons-James J. Corbett fight for the heavyweight championship of the world was scheduled for Dallas in 1895, Culberson listened to the protest of several factions, then announced that this "public display of barbarism" could not be held. The state supreme court ruled there was no law against it. The governor promptly called a special session of the legislature and got a law passed prohibiting prizefighting.

He was so strong for fiscal economy that he vetoed a general appropriation bill, and convened the legislature in special session to approve a measure calling for $400,000 less. He continued to fight against corporate enterprises and large moneyed interests he thought not operating in the public interest.

Culberson was the son of David Browning Culberson, a soldier and statesman who served twenty-two years in the United States Congress, and Eugenia (Kimball) Culberson. He was born in Dadeville, Alabama, on June 19, 1855, and was brought to Texas at the age of one. He married Sallie Harrison in 1882, moved to Dallas in 1887, practiced law, and was elected attorney general of Texas in 1890.

Culberson had a prominent part in framing the war measures of Woodrow Wilson's administration. He remained in Washington after his retirement until his death on March 19, 1925, survived by his wife and a daughter, Mary. He was buried at Fort Worth.

Culberson was a man of relatively few words, but they influenced people and issues.

JOSEPH DRAPER SAYERS
(1899-1903)

Probably no Texas governor so aptly exemplified the old adage that "you can't keep a good man down" as did Joe D. Sayers. During the Civil War he returned to front-line duty on crutches twice after being wounded. He sought and lost the Democratic nomination for governor in 1880, then waited patiently for nearly two decades to make his ambition come true. And once governor, disasters challenged him to prove that you can't keep a good state down, either. For if ever Texas was plagued, it was during his administration.

The Brazos River overflowed in 1899, flooding its valley from McLennan County to the Gulf. The next year brought the worst tragedy in Texas history (other than the Civil War), the Galveston flood. Two years of drought then hit the state, and during this time it dawned on Texas cotton farmers that the boll weevil had come to stay and maybe to destroy Texas' main money crop. Sayers secured millions in aid to help his state recover.

His administration has been described as the passing of the "House of Hogg" and the end of the crusade against monopolies and trusts; the majority of people now felt they had been adequately regulated. Nearly twelve hundred insane persons were transferred from jails and private custody to asylums. Sayers advocated public lands for homestead purposes and the maintenance of efficient public free schools. In spite of the disasters during his tenure, some thirteen hundred miles of railroad were laid in the state, and bank deposits and taxable values rose.

Sayers was born of Celtic ancestry, son of Davis and Mary Thomas (Peete) Sayers, in Grenada, Mississippi, on September 23, 1841, came to Texas with his father in 1851, and attended Bastrop Military Institute. He was commissioned a captain in the Confederate army before he was twenty-one, rose to the rank of major, was admitted to the bar in 1866, and became a member of the state legislature, chairman of the Democratic state executive committee, and lieutenant governor in 1879-1880. He married Orline Walton in 1879, served in the United States Congress from 1885 to 1899, and was governor from 1899 to 1903. He later served as a regent of the University of Texas, and was a member of the Board of Legal Examiners, the Industrial Accident Board, and the Board of Pardon Advisors.

Sayers died May 15, 1929, and was buried at Bastrop. Some observers have designated his administration the connecting link between the Texas of romance and primitive life and the Texas of magnificent development and regal power.

SAMUEL WILLIS TUCKER LANHAM
(1903-1907)

Samuel Willis Tucker Lanham's life in Texas has been described as the "long honeymoon" because he came to Texas on his honeymoon from South Carolina, lived a notably devoted life with his wife, and died heartbroken at her death. But life here was not all orange blossoms. He said he worked himself to death as governor, a lamentation that reminds us of several Spanish governors who wore out under the trials and harassments of the governorship and begged to be relieved ahead of death.

Lanham was born at Spartansburg, South Carolina, on

July 4, 1846. At the age of fifteen, with the Civil War on, he declared he could shoot as well as any man. He was taken at his word and served gallantly in the Virginia campaign. He married Sarah Ming on September 4, 1866, and left for Texas. Five children were born to them. He settled in Red River County, studied law while he taught school, and was admitted to the bar in 1869. Beginning in 1882, he represented the Eleventh District in Congress for over ten years.

Lanham served as governor from 1903 to 1907, a relatively uneventful administration, but he found administering a state much different from representing constituents in the national Congress. Routine chores of the governorship vexed and worried him. As governor he had daily to face old friends seeking favors, many interested in schemes that pulled against his conscience. At sixty he was old, nervous, high-strung, his duties an overwhelming burden. He confined to a friend on retiring: "I made a great mistake when I became governor. . . .Office seekers, pardon seekers, and concession seekers overwhelmed me. They broke my health and when a man finds his health gone, his spirit is broken."

The long honeymoon ended in a nightmare—grief over the death of his beloved wife, whom he had brought to Texas and who had been the daily companion of his life there, brought Lanham unbearable loneliness and fatigue. He followed her a few weeks later, July 29, 1908. The fifteen-year-old Confederate soldier was the last of a long list of Civil War veterans to serve as governor.

THOMAS MITCHELL CAMPBELL
(1907-1911)

Thomas Mitchell Campbell was the first to make the governorship of the state his first political job, and the second governor to be a native of the state. He was born in Cherokee County only a few miles from Jim Hogg's birthplace. It is tradition that the two boys, always fast friends, vowed they would one day become governor. Both were reared in meager circumstances and developed the outlook of the commoner. Twelve years after Hogg's administration, Campbell revived Hogg's political principles.

At the close of Lanham's administration there was a surge toward the policies of Governor Hogg that said the regulation and restriction of corporate powers was a necessity of that time, a departure from the Jeffersonian doctrine that "that government is best which governs least." While the "House of Hogg" had put the laws on the books, Campbell lead a renaissance of stricter and broader enforcement. He procured laws to establish the department of insurance, banking, statistics, and history; the Texas State Library; irrigation and drainage districts; and laws abolishing gambling and leasing prisoners as laborers.

Campbell was born April 22, 1856, son of Thomas Duncan and Rachel (Moore) Campbell. He was so interested in the law that he was often found in the courthouse listening to lawyers when he should have been in school. Because of lack of money he was able to attend only one year at Trinity University, but he worked in the county clerk's office at Longview while he studied law, and was admitted to the bar in 1878. He married Fannie Bruner that same year. From 1893 to 1897 he was general manager of the Great Northern Railroad. He left the job because of his friendship for organized labor.

After Campbell served as governor from 1907 to 1911, he returned to private law practice, ran unsuccessfully for the United States Senate in 1916, died April 1, 1923, and was buried in Palestine. If the story of Tom Campbell's boyhood vow is true, few men ever so accurately accomplish their life's ambition.

OSCAR BRANCH COLQUITT
(1911-1915)

It has been said that Oscar Branch Colquitt had everybody against him except the people, which seems a way of saying that he won individuals but at one time or another had just about every organization in Texas officially fighting him. Because he was a local-option advocate, prohibitionists, ministers, and church groups called him a champion of Demon Rum. Because he was a pro-German propagandist from 1914 to 1916 and an opponent of Woodrow Wilson's Mexican policy, Wilson supporters challenged his patriotism. He had little confrontations as well as big ones. The Daughters of the Confederacy tangled with him over possession of office room under the Big Dome, while the Daughters of the Republic needled him no end about who should be guardian of the battlefield shrines of the state. And so it went. He just was not one to kowtow, or be overly impressed by titled, organized power.

He knew how to impress individuals, and how to utilize imagery rather than abstractions. He was against torture punishment in the prisons and convict farms. To get his message to the voters, he campaigned the state with a big bullwhip in his hand. After a thunderous crack with it, at which he was an expert, he asked the voters if they would sustain by their ballot that implement of human torture. Colquitt had the vital political insight that voters feel about issues more easily and quickly than they reason about them.

During his administration, the first eighteen-hour labor law was passed. In addition, laws regulating child and woman labor, workmen's compensation, and home rule for cities over five thousand went on the statute books.

Colquitt was born December 16, 1861, at Camilla, Georgia, son of Thomas Jefferson and Ann Elizabeth (Burk-

Samuel Willis Tucker Lanham
1903-1907

Thomas Mitchell Campbell
1907-1911

Oscar Branch Colquitt
1911-1915

James E. Ferguson
1915-1917

halter) Colquitt. The family moved to Dangerfield, Texas, in 1878. Young Colquitt worked at a number of jobs—tenant farmer, hod carrier, railway porter, maker of bedposts in a furniture factory, and printer's devil. He later owned and operated his own newspaper. As an editor he realized his chief interest was politics, so he studied law and was admitted to the bar in 1900. He had married Alice Fuller Murrell in 1885, and they in time became the parents of five children.

He served as state senator beginning in 1895, railroad commissioner from 1903 to 1911, and governor from 1911 to 1915. After the governorship he served as president of a Dallas oil company, member of the United States Board of Mediation, and from 1935 to his death, March 8, 1940, field representative of the Reconstruction Finance Corporation.

Colquitt's close friends referred to him as "Little Oscar"; those not so close called him "the Napoleon of Texas politics." He was a "self-made" man, obstinate though affable, not a polished orator but a colorful, effective stump speaker who in his own particular way accomplished what he thought needed doing.

JAMES E. FERGUSON
(1915-1917)

James E. "Farmer Jim" Ferguson, it is generally agreed, was Texas' most colorful and controversial governor other than Sam Houston. He was impeached at the beginning of his second term, but was, for long periods afterward, the most influential politician in Texas.

Even as a youth Jim was colorful. He was born near Salado on August 31, 1871. His father died about the time he turned five, leaving the family, he said, "as poor as

Job's turkey." His education was limited to a short acquaintance with the "blueback" speller, McGuffey's reader, and Ray's arithmetic, "between crops." At sixteen he tramped over the West working at whatever odd jobs he could find to make a living—bellboy in Denver, hop picker in California, bridge hand on Texas railroads.

He returned home and studied law for a brief time. Some things came hard for Jim Ferguson, but not his admittance to the bar. The usual procedure for an aspirant to the law was to study under a member of the profession for a few months to three years, and then be examined by a committee of members of the bar appointed by a court judge. If he passed, the clerk of court was ordered to issue him a certificate to practice. When Ferguson appeared for examination in 1897, he was not asked a single question, according to his biographer, O. W. Nalle. The examining judge, after passing a drink of whiskey around to the committee, said: "This boy's father, Parson Ferguson, was the best friend the young lawyers of Bell County ever had. I move you, gentlemen, that his son, Jim, be given a license to practice law in Texas."

One member replied that he could not get along with his conscience if he did not ask him a single legal question.

"There you go with your conscience," the judge snapped. "Suppose Jim couldn't answer the question, how could you get along with your conscience?"

Whatever his preparation in law, he made enough money at it to invest in rich farmlands, and between the two, to establish the Temple State Bank.

In 1914 he entered the governor's race entirely on his own without a campaign manager. As governor, he put an end to prohibition agitation by vetoing all laws for or against the liquor traffic. State aid to rural schools was begun, a compulsory school attendance law passed, three new normal schools authorized, a highway department created, and bonded warehouses established. Ferguson's pet measure curbed tenant farmers' rent to a third of the grain and a fourth of the cotton, and half and half division of the produce when the landlord furnished everything.

Ferguson may not have been a hating man, for one of his most descriptive quotations was "If I hated just one person, I wouldn't have time to do anything else." In view of his lasting political power, he obviously forgave his enemies, and learned to use more temperate language in his later days. If he did not hate some University of Texas professors, he had a fatal dislike for them. When the board of regents failed to remove them on his request, he vetoed practically the entire appropriation for the university. In a blazing speech on the subject, he shouted, "Some people have not only gone hog wild but become damn fools over the idea that we must have an army of educated fools to run the government."

This squabble with the university people started the movement toward impeachment. The charges of impeachment are too involved and controversial for treatment here. Suffice it to say that they put Ferguson out of office, but ironically not out of political leadership.

Though ineligible to hold office, he sought the Democratic nomination for governor in 1918 and lost. In 1920 he ran unsuccessfully for president, and in 1922 ran unsuccessfully for the United States Senate. However, in 1924 and 1932 he conducted successful campaigns for his wife's election to the governorship.

Ferguson died September 24, 1944, and was buried in the State Cemetery in Austin. Because of the color and excitement surrounding him, he is one of Texas' most widely known governors.

WILLIAM P. HOBBY
(1917-1921)

William P. Hobby started as low in the newspaper business as one could and went about as high. He started as a janitor-clerk for the *Houston Post*, and not many years later he owned it. His career in politics was relatively short. It has been said that he was reluctant to get involved and eager to get out.

He was born at Moscow, Texas, on March 26, 1878, son of Edwin and Eudora Adeline (Pettus) Hobby. After attending high school in Houston, he went to work for the *Houston Post* in 1895, and within a few years became its managing editor. In 1907 he became editor and publisher of the *Beaumont Enterprise* and the *Beaumont Journal*.

Hobby was elected lieutenant governor in 1914, becoming governor when James Ferguson was impeached in 1917. In 1918 he defeated Ferguson for governor by a large majority. His administration dealt mainly with problems of World War I, a severe drought, and the improvement of education and roads.

After completing his term he never sought public office again, though he maintained a deep interest in governmental affairs. He returned to the *Beaumont Enterprise*, bought the *Beaumont Journal*, and was associated with both papers until 1924 when he returned to the *Houston Post*, which he later bought and which from then on was his chief business interest.

In 1915 Hobby married Willie Chapman Cooper, who died in 1929. He married Oveta Culp, parliamentarian of the Texas House of Representatives, in 1931.

Friends remember Will Hobby as a friendly, modest, smiling man of ready wit and tireless energy. The title of his chief biography appropriately tags him "The Tactful Texan." He died June 6, 1964.

William P. Hobby
1917-1921

Pat M. Neff
1921-1925

The Hobby touch is yet on the face of the state and nation. His wife, Mrs. Oveta Culp Hobby, nationally known for such positions as director of the Women's Army Corps, is still at the helm of the influential *Houston Post*. His son, William Hobby, Jr., was elected lieutenant governor of Texas in 1972.

PAT M. NEFF
(1921-1925)

When Pat M. Neff was running for governor, he boasted that he had never tasted tea, coffee, tobacco, or liquor. He depended upon handshaking and the personal touch rather than oratory. His campaign was strenuous—he electioneered in thirty-seven counties where no candidate for governor had ever personally solicited votes before—but probably no candidate ever enjoyed campaigning more. His platform was as simple and vague as it was effective: "to make Texas a better place to live in." Everybody could understand such a noble motive. And who could argue against it?

He didn't bother much about specifics. So planks in the platforms of the opposition were details more inclined to confuse the people than make them feel comfortable. Neff represented goodness, brotherly love—the ole-time religion. Most convincing of all, he practiced what he preached. It was easy for voters to believe that Pat Neff and God stood for the same things.

Neff was born at McGregor, Texas, on November 26, 1871, son of Noah and Isabella (Shepherd) Neff. He married Myrtle Mainer of Lovelady in 1899. He took A.B. and M.A. degrees from Baylor and a law degree from the University of Texas. He practiced law at Waco and served six years as McLennan County prosecuting attorney and four

years in the Texas legislature, two of them as speaker of
the House. He became governor in 1921 and served two
terms. As governor he stressed development of Texas' state
park system, abolition of the Board of Pardons, development of educational institutions and industries, and ad-
vance planning for the Texas Centennial.

After leaving the governor's office, he returned to the
practice of law, served on the Board of Mediation in 1927-
1929, and was chairman of the Texas Railroad Commission in 1929-1931. He served as president of Baylor University from 1932 to 1947, and was active in many religious
and fraternal organizations—president of the Baptist General Convention of Texas, the Southern Baptist Convention, grand master of Texas Masons, and so on.

Pat Neff died January 20, 1952, at Waco. He had
worked hard and seriously at many things, and seems to
have enjoyed them all.

MIRIAM A. FERGUSON
(1925-1927, 1933-1935)

In the closing paragraph of *Texas Governors' Wives* the
author said of Mrs. Miriam A. Ferguson, after her husband
became governor, "She is but started in her life in the
Mansion"—a prophecy of such magnitude and accuracy
that few Texans could have envisioned. She presided at the
Mansion for nearly seven years during part of two terms of
her husband's administration and two of her own, a record
to that time. She was controversial, and like her husband,
Jim, colorful in a folksy way.

Not many people were neutral about the Fergusons—"Ma" and "Pa," as they came to be called. Few
personalities ever divided Texas as did the Fergusons. Possibly no more determined people ever lived in the Mansion.

Miriam A. Ferguson
1925-1927
1933-1935

Dan Moody
1927-1931

Nothing seemed to faze them—criticism, slander, even impeachment and disbarment from office.

Miriam Ferguson was born in Bell County, Texas, on June 13, 1875, daughter of Joseph and Eliza (Garrison) Wallace. She was reared on a farm, attended Salado College and Baylor Belton College for Women (but did not graduate), and on the last day of the nineteenth century married James E. Ferguson, a distant relative. They had two daughters.

Her campaign for governor in 1924 was sensational and heated. Charges and countercharges flew. During the campaign Ma appeared about as folksy as one could get, even in the rural Texas of that time. On the campaign trail she wore a sunbonnet in the shadow of Pa.

Not enough time has passed to evaluate this determined, hurt couple, calling on the people to set aright a great wrong by voting their confidence in them. People from the country could not understand how "intellectuals" could possibly call a gracious, country-reared, sympathetic-acting, middle-aged lady in a sunbonnet a phony. When opponents charged that she was a political stooge, she replied sweetly that when she was elected, Texas would have two governors for the price of one. No question about it—somewhere in the Ferguson camp was a master of catch phrases that could make the crowds whoop, and no logic could prevail against them. The Fergusons were underdogs, and there was something noble and terribly appealing about a Texas woman of pioneer stock in a sunbonnet challenging the mightiest of political stalwarts in defense of her husband's honor. She was against booze, the Ku Klux Klan, and the selfish, meddling big business moguls who didn't care for or understand common folks "like us." And she had motherhood on her side.

Mrs. Ferguson assumed the governorship early in 1925, and left many of the details of the office to her husband.

If Mrs. Ferguson's election, in the Fergusons' opinion, showed up the impeaching legislature as not representing the will of the people, or doing justice to husband Jim, they were ready to emphasize the point to the full measure. Mrs. Ferguson ran to succeed herself but was defeated by Dan Moody. She ran again in 1930 against another stalwart, Ross R. Sterling, and was defeated. Defeats the Fergusons were used to, and as hard to discourage as they came. She took on Governor Ross Sterling again and squeaked out a victory to become governor once more in 1933.

There were no great, compelling issues during these administrations. Husband Jim, during the campaign of 1932, made a summary of what Fergusonism meant by listing some laws passed: laws regulating working hours for women, compulsory school laws, free textbook law, regulation of employment agencies, semimonthly paydays for workers, aid for rural education, workmen's compensation law, child labor law, establishment of certain colleges, and so on. Some opponents have argued over whether some of these "accomplishments" were achieved because of, or in spite of, the Fergusons.

Mrs. Ferguson died June 25, 1961. Doubtless nowhere has there been so close and controversial a wife-husband team in high places. It perhaps will be talked about as long as there is a Texas.

DAN MOODY
(1927-1931)

Red-haired Dan Moody was the youngest man to become governor of the state of Texas up to that time. His race for the governor's office has been called the "honeymoon campaign," because soon after he announced his candidacy, he married Miss Mildred Paxton of Abilene, and he made the campaign with his happy, smiling bride by his side. It gave a romantic touch to an otherwise bitter campaign against the Fergusons.

Moody was born June 1, 1893, at Taylor, son of Daniel J. and Nancy Elizabeth (Robertson) Moody. His father was sixty when Dan was born, and dead when Dan was fifteen. Dan helped his mother run a dairy, was delivery boy for drugstores, and worked at setting telegraph poles, then stringing wire. He graduated from the law department at the University of Texas, practiced law, and became a prosecuting attorney. He gained nationwide publicity by getting the first conviction in a Ku Klux Klan flogging case, which put the floggers in the penitentiary and Moody in the attorney general's office. As attorney general, he collected large sums of money proved overpaid to highway contractors.

He won the governorship in 1926 at the age of thirty-three. He reformed the Highway Commission, instituted a statewide campaign against crime, put the state prisons under new and more rigid management, and reversed the Ferguson liberal pardoning policies.

At the author's request, Mrs. Dan Moody contributed some of her recollections about her husband and his work: "He gained notoriety for unmasking the crooked highway deals . . . I think his greatest contribution was the feeling people had that Dan Moody put HONESTY and fair-dealing back into public office. . . . He was so honest he did not make a 'good politician.'. . . The government was so riddled with prior appointments . . . that Dan was unable to get rid of much of the rottenness in the state organization . . . Dan did clean out the Highway Department, which was in a terrible state. . . . you may say he was responsible for the real beginning of the finest highway set-up of the nation. . . ."

After retiring from office in 1931, he returned to the practice of law at Austin. Dan Moody died May 22, 1966— a man who started young enough to give his most vigorous years to the chief needs of Texas.

ROSS S. STERLING
(1931-1933)

Ross Sterling, the first "big business" man to become governor of Texas, was the founder and first president of the Humble Oil and Refining Company, a real estate developer, and owner of the *Post-Dispatch* of Houston, which later became the *Houston Post*. He built a railroad and was one of the guiding spirits behind the construction of the Houston ship channel. In his time he served as president of the Sterling Oil and Refining Company, president of American Maid Flour Mills and the Ross Sterling Investment Company, and chairman of the board of the Houston National Bank.

Ross S. Sterling, son of Benjamin Franklin and Mary Jane (Byran) Sterling, was born in February, 1875, at Anahuac, almost in sight of the place where Texas was born—San Jacinto. He went to public schools and farmed until about 1896.

He served under Governor Moody as chairman of the Highway Commission. He ran for governor on his record for cleaning up this department and was elected in 1930. His were mainly the problems of the Depression. He called a special session of the legislature to pass a law to cut cotton acreage fifty percent. It did, but the law was declared unconstitutional. Because rulings of the Texas Railroad Commission regulating oil proration in East Texas were being ignored, he placed four counties under martial law and shut down oil production for a time. The courts

Ross S. Sterling
1931-1933

James V. Allred
1935-1939

ruled that he had exceeded his authority.

The Depression brought not only official problems but personal ones as well. His public service was rendered at great personal sacrifice. While struggling with problems of state, he neglected his personal affairs and lost his fortune. In 1932 he was defeated by Mrs. Ferguson by a little over four thousand votes, and set out at making another fortune—in oil and agriculture.

Sterling married Maud Abbie Gage in 1898, and fathered five children. His second fortune was sufficient for him to participate in several philanthropies.

He was a big man, more than six feet tall and weighing about two hundred fifty pounds. He died March 25, 1949, and was buried in Houston. Ross Sterling was a Horatio Alger hero come to life.

JAMES V. ALLRED
(1935-1939)

James V. Allred was known as the "Centennial Governor" because his signature to legislation made the celebration of 1936 possible, and his promotion brought national attention to it and Texas. He was as much a do-it-yourself man as any to become governor, and was as "calculating" about it. His is a story of accomplishment—a quality not given but self-made.

Allred not only knew what he wanted to do, but he let others know. During navy days when a group of comrades were talking about what they were going to do when the war was over, he said emphatically, "I'm going back home and run for governor."

He was born at Bowie on March 29, 1899, son of Mary Magdalene (Henson) and Rene Allred, a rural mail carrier. A boy couldn't start any closer to the bottom than Jimmie

Allred did. He sold newspapers, shined shoes, worked as a janitor, and ran errands to help pay for his schooling, but he got schooling in spite of war and lack of money. He enrolled at Rice Institute (now Rice University) in 1917, but a year later left his classes and enlisted in the United States Navy.

After the war he was still on a low rung of the ladder, but as ever, not discouraged. He worked as a stenographer for a law firm in Wichita Falls for a while, then entered Cumberland University, graduated with a law degree in 1921, and took up the practice of law in Wichita Falls. He became a district attorney, and at the age of thirty-one was attorney general. He married Joe Betsy Miller of Wichita Falls in 1927; they had three sons.

He was inaugurated governor in January, 1935, and served two terms. At the author's request, Mrs. Joe Betsy Allred listed what she considered some of the most important achievements of her late husband. They are so succinctly and clearly phrased as to merit quoting as a first-hand public record:

> . . . as attorney-general he made a record fight against business monopolies and against corporations to influence state taxation. He defended oil production laws. He established for the state school fund its title to West Texas oil royalties worth over $20,000,000.
>
> As governor, he took the lead in setting up a teachers' retirement fund, and he attempted to attain fairer salaries for educators.
>
> He set up a Board of Pardons and Paroles to determine the fate of prisoners. He instituted prison reforms.
>
> He signed into law the state's first unemployment insurance measure.

He combined the Texas Rangers and the Highway Patrol in trying to curb vice and lawlessness.

He put an end to pari-mutual betting in Texas.

He signed into law the first old age assistance bill for Texans.

During his tenure, social security amendments were added to the State Constitution.

In 1942 Allred ran unsuccessfully for the United States Senate against W. Lee O'Daniel. He was appointed judge of the United States District Court in 1951 by Harry Truman. He died September 24, 1959.

James V. Allred knew what he wanted to do, and believing he could do it, did—revealing that self-confidence inspires public confidence.

W. LEE O'DANIEL
(1939-1941)

W. Lee O'Daniel was Texas' great showman. He was Barnum and Bailey and Joe Miller all in one tall, handsome package with an irresistible voice and disarming grin. Old-line politicians had reason to be disturbed when this sensational flour salesman moved onto the political stage to sell himself to the voters rather than flour to housewives. He was an announced hillbilly, made up to appeal to the common people. Who needed the others? As he proved by mowing down more political stalwarts than any other man of his time.

Once elected governor, he put on the most glamorous and dazzling show for his inauguration ever seen in Texas. It required the University of Texas football stadium to hold the assembly, estimated at up to seventy-five thousand people. At least a hundred uniformed bands played, and the fanfare and pomp and pageantry could not have failed to give the impression that something great and exciting and unforgettable was happening to Texas. If his administration could not live up to his glorious pledges and the high pitch of his inauguration ceremonies, at least now everybody in Texas knew who their governor was.

He disappointed some friends and partisans by not always being able to fulfill his promises, but he kept right on entertaining the people and telling his side of the story, just as he did when he was peddling flour by radio. When he was feuding with the legislature, he delivered "sermons" and "fireside chats" from the governor's mansion on Sunday mornings by radio until the home folk had to believe that even if not always a good governor, he was a "good guy," and that was what really counted.

In times of campaigns and controversy, he took to the open road with his hillbilly band. He wrote songs and poetry. His troupe performed to entertain crowds that blocked his path to hear him. As an entertainer with a politician's true sense of fundamentals, he knew what the voters *felt* was important. Let the amateurs and idealists spout philosophy, tear their brains to convince the people of what they needed, and shout their leather lungs to threads in the effort to make the voters *think*. He just sang "The Boy Who Never Gets Too Big to Comb His Mother's Hair," "Your Own Sweet Darling Wife," and "Beautiful Texas." With such songs spiritedly accompanied by guitar and fiddle, nobody could forget for a minute that he was all out for Motherhood, God, and Country.

His stated platform was the Ten Commandments and the Golden Rule. Thus he was clearly against the devil to the last, and against Johnson grass for sure, season by season.

O'Daniel was born in Malta, Ohio, on March 11, 1890, son of William Barnes and Alice Ann (Thompson) O'Daniel.

He was reared in Kansas, where he graduated from a business college in 1908 and became a stenographer for a flour milling company. He stayed in the flour business, mainly as a salesman, until he became president of the Burrus Mill and Elevator Company. With his Light-Crust Doughboys hillbilly band, his homespun philosophy, and his superb salesmanship, he decided to concentrate on selling himself instead of flour. In 1938 he defeated eleven candidates to become governor, and won reelection two years later, the first gubernatorial candidate to receive a million votes.

Following the death of United States Senator Morris Sheppard, he called a special election and announced his candidacy for the position. The politicians of Texas even now could not believe the power of the O'Daniel magic. Twenty-six candidates lined up against him in the race, but nothing could prevail against such surefire vote getters as "Pass the Biscuits, Pappy," and "Pappy" was fiddled and yodeled right out of Austin straight into the United States Senate.

A magazine of his day observed that O'Daniel's "unfamiliarity with governmental and economic problems handicapped him at every turn and his legislative program bogged down." He, in the main, blamed the legislature, and as a whole they were glad enough to have him in Washington. Historians find it much easier to evaluate him as an entertainer than as a statesman.

His reelection to the Senate was a mere formality. About as flushed with success as one could get, he was colorful and persistent, one of the most artful public relations men who ever got into politics. There was a good deal of talk about him running for president, but Roosevelt seemed to have a permanent lease on the White House, and the great showman had finally found a man he couldn't fiddle down. O'Daniel retired voluntarily from the Senate in 1949, and returned to Texas to live a relatively quiet life.

In June, 1917, he had married Merle Estella Butcher, to whom were born three children. All of them played musical instruments and helped promote the O'Daniel image.

Once the professional politicians saw that O'Daniel could sell himself as surely as he could sell a sack of flour, they would have done well to save their registration and campaign fees. But to the politicians he was the red flag in the matador's hands, so the best of them charged him and went down like tenpins until Texas finally exhausted itself in its own political excitement, or else the great ringmaster had tired of it all himself and decided to pop his whip no more.

O'Daniel died in May, 1969. He may have been the best and last of his breed. Nobody else in Texas ever had quite the charisma, the brass, the surefire formula, to sell himself so consistently so long.

COKE R. STEVENSON
(1941-1947)

Coke Stevenson will be remembered as "the last representative of the true Texas pioneer strain to sit in the Governor's chair," wrote a close observer of this rancher-governor who liked to cook his own breakfast and get to the executive office by six in the morning. At the capitol he looked more the rancher than the chief executive—tall and wiry, erect, often in cowboy boots, a man who appeared designed more for a saddle than a swivel chair.

In office he practiced the rugged individualism of the self-reliant pioneers who asked of government mainly to stay out of the way. From the federal government he wanted neither aid nor meddling. He believed that industry, thrift, and integrity would succeed "as they always

W. Lee O'Daniel
1939-1941

Coke R. Stevenson
1941-1947

have," and that bureaucratic coddling would paralyze the economy and make a hardy people soft and flabby.

He was born in a log hut in Mason County on March 20, 1888. His grandfather was a circuit-riding Methodist preacher, and his father a self-taught schoolteacher and surveyor who was a "pretty fair fiddler."

Coke said he never had time to learn to play the fiddle. He had to work. At the age of fourteen he completed his formal education of twenty-two months of one-room schoolhouse learning and went to work as a ranch hand until he saved enough to buy a freight wagon and six horses. He began hauling freight (mainly coffins) from Junction to Brady. At night beside his cargo he studied bookkeeping by the light of his campfire, and then slept on the ground. After "graduating" from his correspondence course, he applied for a position at a Junction bank, not as a bookkeeper but as floor sweeper and custodian of the cuspidors. But in less than two years he was a cashier. Again at night he continued his education, this time in law. On Christmas Eve, 1912, he married Fay Wright, and they began housekeeping in a home he had built with his own hands from salvaged lumber. The next year he passed the bar examination.

He became president of a bank and built an abstracting business and a theater—all this along with politics. He was county attorney, then county judge, and in 1928 ran successfully for the legislature, where he became speaker of the House for two terms. He was elected lieutenant governor in 1938, was reelected, then became governor when O'Daniel resigned to become United States senator. Stevenson was elected governor twice.

His administration was dominated by the principle of status quo: let good enough alone. Some of his friends thought he was too taciturn, that he should have spoken out stronger on some issues. He may have been too cautious at times about risking misunderstanding, depending too much upon his friends' knowing where he stood. He once said, "Blessed is he who sayeth nothing for he shall not be misquoted."

A self-made man who grew up in lean times, he carried his frugal habits to the capitol. As governor he was known to have walked back up the capitol stairs to make sure he had turned off his office lights. It startled him to learn that some governors had chauffeurs and limousines. He traveled about Austin in an old-model blue Ford. His one noticeable luxury was smoking pipes. He had about two hundred of them, a hundred fifty received as gifts while he was governor.

After the governorship he ran for the United States Senate, and lost to Lyndon B. Johnson by less than a hundred votes in one of the most puzzling elections in Texas history. He retired to the serenity of his vast ranch near Junction—not bitter, not a recluse—to work hard, as he had always done, to read, to live in harmony with the earth and the people he knew best, and to "practice a little law" for his neighbors, without as much as a telephone to connect him with a more turbulent world. He died June 28, 1975.

Coke Stevenson was a sentinel crying out against government pampering and bureaucracy, which his ever-diminishing breed of self-reliant individualist thinks is crushing the free spirit of America.

BEAUFORD HALBERT JESTER
(1947-1949)

Beauford Halbert Jester was Mr. Middle-of-the-Road, about as average, in many respects, as a man might be and be a governor. His background was much that way, neither noticeably aristocratic nor underprivileged. His ancestors had fought in the wars for America and taken part in forming governments. He was well grounded in the basic American traditions. His folk were civic and religious leaders. At the time he was governor, his mother boasted that she had taught a Sunday-school class for over sixty years.

Beauford Halbert Jester, son of George Taylor and Frances (Gordon) Jester, was born January 12, 1893, in Corsicana, and reared there. As a youngster he operated a soda-water stand and delivered milk to earn money. He took B.A. and LL.B. degrees from the University of Texas. He served in World War I, where he was called "Captain Kid" by his older troopers, was admitted to the bar in June, 1920, was appointed a member of the Railroad Commission in 1942, and ran without opposition for a term beginning January 1, 1945.

He ran a heated race, centering around Homer P. Rainey, ousted president of the University of Texas seeking vindication, to become governor in 1947. During his administration, the Gilmer-Akin law, which reorganized the public schools, was passed. Laws were passed prohibiting picketing public utilities if such was intended to disrupt public services. A "right to work" bill was passed along with other labor laws.

If Jester did not show great originality, and risk going out on political limbs, he showed knowledge of what had worked as people-winners in the past. Like Governor Neff, he formulated his creeds to irreducible simplicity and comprehensiveness: He was for government "of the people, by the people, and for the people." And "Our government . . . must always be mindful that the Home, the Church, and the School are the very foundations of our well-being and ever strive to strengthen these foundations." Certainly there was safety in his method. No opponent could successfully attack his stand on such sacred institutions on either principle or announced intent. And one could hardly damage a politician by attacking him for triteness.

Jester married Mabel Buchanan in 1921, and to them two daughters were born. He was a member of many civic, fraternal, and religious organizations.

He was elected to succeed himself, but died July 11, 1949, before finishing his first term, and was buried in Corsicana. Jester, apparently to the extent that he could, stuck to the tried and ordinary, and for him it worked beyond the ordinary.

ALLAN SHIVERS
(1949-1957)

If Allan Shivers was not naturally endowed with qualities for leadership, he soon developed them. He was endowed with a striking physique, all six feet two inches and two hundred pounds of it. He developed interests in many things, and an unbounding energy brought him success in many endeavors. His friends were glad one of his numerous interests was politics.

Born October 5, 1907, at Lufkin, son of Robert Andrew and Ester (Creasy) Shivers, he spent most of his early years near Woodville and Port Arthur. They were busy, versatile years. He sold shoes and worked at a sawmill, at the State Treasury, and at a petroleum refinery. He obtained a law degree from the University of Texas, and began the practice of law at Port Arthur in 1931. At the age of twenty-seven he was elected to the Texas Senate, probably the youngest person elected to serve in that body thus far. He was reelected twice. Beginning in 1943, he served two years in World War II and was dis-

Beauford Halbert Jester
1947-1949

Allan Shivers
1949-1957

charged with the rank of major.

He was elected lieutenant governor in 1946 and 1948. When Governor Jester died in 1949, Shivers became governor and was reelected to three successive terms, giving him the longest administration of anyone up to that time.

On his birthday in 1937, he married Marialice Shary, daughter of a pioneer developer of the citrus industry in the Rio Grande Valley. They are the parents of two sons and a daughter. Rancher, farmer, lawyer, statesman, businessman, Shivers is still interested in many enterprises, including banking, savings and loans, airlines, insurance, sulphur, and oil. He holds honorary degrees from several universities, and remains active in civic affairs.

Still with abundant energy, broad interests and perception in many fields, no one can anticipate the finis to Shivers' biography.

PRICE DANIEL
(1957-1963)

When this writer first met Price Daniel on one of his early campaigns, Daniel gave the impression of an unpretentious, sincere man asking the voters for a job he felt qualified to handle—a man aiming for statesmanship in the best Texas tradition. And that's about the way it has been. Few Texans have spent more of their life in public service in so many capacities. Thus space will permit little more than a listing of his main accomplishments.

Marion Price Daniel was born in Dayton, Texas, on October 10, 1910, son of Marion and Nannie (Partlow) Daniel. He took degrees in journalism and law at Baylor University, and began the practice of law in Liberty in

1932. He has been a man of varied interests, organizing a jazz band at Baylor, showing his talent early for politics by being elected president of his class, and later becoming co-owner and publisher of the *Liberty Vindicator* and the *Anahuac Progress*.

He served three terms as a member of the Texas House of Representatives, and was elected speaker of the House during his last term. He enlisted in the army in 1943 as a private and was discharged in 1946 as a captain. He served three terms as attorney general, smashing the Maceo gambling syndicate, and fought for Texas' rights to the tidelands.

Daniel was elected United States senator in 1952 and served four years. Here he coauthored the bill that restored to Texas its three million acres of submerged lands in the Gulf of Mexico. During his three terms as governor, beginning in 1957, he argued the boundary case in which Texas' title and three-league boundary were upheld by the United States Supreme Court. In 1967 and 1968 he served as assistant to the president of the United States for federal-state relations, as director of the Office of Emergency Preparedness, and as a member of the National Security Council. He was appointed to the Texas Supreme Court on January 1, 1971, where he is presently serving.

Judge Daniel is a writer by education and experience. His publications include *Texas Election Laws, Texas Publication Laws*, and *Executive Mansions and Capitals of America*, coauthored by Mrs. Daniel. His *Report to the Legislature, 1957-1963*, gives a valuable account of that period. In 1940 he married Jean Houston, a descendant of Sam Houston, and they are the parents of four children.

The long, distinguished public service of Price Daniel yet continues.

Price Daniel
1957-1963

John B. Connally
1963-1969

JOHN B. CONNALLY
(1963-1969)

No Texas governor has ever set a more distinguished record for service in so many high places than John B. Connally. His service has reached beyond party politics.

He was born February 27, 1917, in Floresville, Texas, son of John Bowden and Lela (Wright) Connally. His talent for leadership was early recognized and called on. He headed several student organizations at the University of Texas, where he earned a law degree. He served as secretary to Representative Lyndon Johnson in Washington in 1939, then enlisted in the navy in 1941 as an ensign. He was many times decorated, and by 1945 was a lieutenant commander.

After the war Connally was administrative assistant to Senator Lyndon Johnson, member of a law firm, and engaged in numerous business enterprises, including management of broadcasting, real estate, oil and gas, ranching, manufacturing, and investment interests. He became secretary of the navy in the John F. Kennedy administration, January 26, 1961, but later resigned to run for governor of Texas. He served in that capacity for three terms, beginning in 1963. On November 22, 1963, Governor Connally was critically wounded while riding with President Kennedy when the president was assassinated in Dallas.

Many political and civic groups have called on him to be their leader: Caucus of Democratic Governors in 1964, Southern Governors' Conference in 1965, and Interstate Oil Compact Commission in 1965, to mention a few. He served on President Nixon's Advisory Council on Executive Organization in 1969-1970, and as a member of the Foreign Intelligence Advisory Board from December 1, 1970, until he was appointed secretary of the treasury on February 11, 1971—a position he held until June 12,

1972, when he resigned to return to private life.

Connally served again under Nixon as a member of the Foreign Intelligence Advisory Board from August 1, 1972, to late 1974. During mid-1973 he served as special advisor to the president. After resigning his post in Washington, he resumed law practice in Houston. He is a director in numerous business and civic organizations.

In 1940 he married Idanell Brill, the University of Texas sweetheart of 1938. They have three children.

Few people of the nation have shown such a comprehensive grasp of so many complex problems and been so articulate in analyzing them in the light of the public good. His candor and openness have become a trademark of that basic quality for leadership—confidence in character and ability.

He has been spoken of often as a presidential candidate. In view of the record, there cannot be much room for speculation about the man himself. The needs of the country and the perception of the people in the light of these needs doubtless will determine his future course.

PRESTON SMITH
(1969-1973)

When Preston Smith was eight years old, he told his mother that he had decided to become governor of Texas. The mother of a houseful of children had little time to discuss the governorship with an eight-year-old, and doubtless shrugged off the announcement as childish pratter. But when Smith actually became governor fifty years later, he explained it this way: "I set the goal as a kid and never lost sight of it."

The boy had a long way to go. He was born in William-

Preston Smith
1969-1973

Dolph Briscoe, Jr.
1973-

son County on March 8, 1912, the seventh of thirteen children in a poor tenant family. His parents, Charles Kirby and Effie Mae Smith, had little to offer a boy setting out to be governor, so he had to make his own way. When the farm work was done he trapped skunks and coyotes for their pelts, and later worked in a filling station to put himself through college. He graduated from Texas Technological College in 1934 with a degree in business administration, then started in business as a service station operator, and later operated a motion picture theater, which he developed into a chain.

With his eyes ever on the governorship, he took one of the most common routes to the Mansion: he became state representative, 1944-1950; state senator, 1957-1963; and lieutenant governor, 1963-1967. He realized his long dream in 1969 when he became governor—to last until 1973. His legislative program included teacher pay raises, better training and pay for law enforcement personnel, a minimum wage law, increased workmen's compensation, work-release plan for prisoners, and implementation of the statewide water plan.

In 1935 Smith married Ima Mae Smith, whom he had conveniently met, thanks to alphabetical seating arrangements, while both were in the same class in college. They are the parents of a son and a daughter.

He has been described as a "rough-hewn," "dead-earnest," methodical man, not flamboyant or colorful, a man who talks down-to-earth common sense rather than relying on oratory. He currently lives in Lubbock, and is a member of numerous civic and fraternal organizations.

Long-range planning, ambition, determination, and unreserved energy are ingredients for turning dreams into reality. Preston Smith put the ingredients together.

DOLPH BRISCOE, JR.
(1973-)

Dolph Briscoe, Jr., rancher-businessman, rose to the governorship via four terms in the state legislature.

He was born in Uvalde, Texas, on April 23, 1923. His mother was a Briscoe, a distant relative of his father. He graduated at the head of his high school class in 1939, took a degree at the University of Texas in 1943, served in the China-Burma-India theater during World War II, and was in the legislature from 1949 to 1957. He became governor in 1973.

Measures that Briscoe favors for improvement include better control and supervision over state finances, crime prevention and control, emphasis on career training for students and older citizens to equip them for earning a living and provide vocational training for youngsters not planning to attend college, insurance reform, implementation of a statewide water plan—one that would move water to West Texas from areas of surplus outside of the state—state assistance to cities and counties for developing mass transit facilities, and developing tourism and industry. He proposed a mobile field office, a sort of traveling branch of the governor's office, to visit Texas communities to listen to local needs.

Briscoe married Janey Slaughter in 1942. Besides holding public office, he has been active in civic affairs. He was president of the Texas and Southwestern Cattle Raisers Association in 1960 and 1961, and president of the Texas State Chamber of Commerce in 1967 and 1968. Some of the many honors awarded him include the Kapp-Porter Award for distinguished service to agriculture, being named Mr. South Texas in 1967 and Outstanding Conservation Rancher in Texas in 1958, an honorary Doctor of Law degree, and numerous awards for service in the

Boy Scout movement.

His leadership is sought by many organizations. He is a former chairman and/or trustee of numerous organizations, including the Mohair Council of America, Southwest Animal Health Research Foundation (he was a leader in the movement to eliminate the screw worm through sterilization of male flies), National Livestock and Meat Board, Texas A & M Research Foundation, and San Antonio Livestock Foundation.

Dolph Briscoe is young enough to still have a future. The eyes of Texas are very much upon him.

Roster of Governors

Rene Robert Cavelier, Sieur de La Salle   1685-1687
Sieur Barbier   1687-1689

SPANISH PERIOD

Domingo Teran de los Rios   1691-1692
Martin de Alarcon   1716-1719
Marques de San Miguel de Aguayo   1719-1722
Fernando Perez de Almazan   1722-
Juan Antonio Bustillo y Zevallos   1731-1734?
Manuel de Sandoval   1734-1736
Carlos Franquis de Lugo   1736-1737
Joseph Fernandez de Jauregui y Urrutia   1737
Prudencio de Orobio y Basterra   1737-1741
Thomas Felipe Wintuisen   1741-1743
Justo Boneo y Morales   1743-1744
Francisco Garcia Larios   1744-1748
Pedro del Barrio Junco y Espriella   1748-1750
Jacinto de Barrios y Jauregui   1751-1759
Angel de Martos y Navarrete   1759-1766

Hugo Oconor   1767-1770
Juan Maria Vicencio de Ripperda,
    Baron de Ripperda   1770-1778
Domingo Cabello   1778-1786
Rafael Martinez Pacheco   1787-1790
Manuel Munoz   1790-1799
Juan Bautista Elguezabal   1799-1805
Manuel Antonio Cordero y Bustamante   1805-1808
Manuel Maria de Salcedo   1808-1813
Juan Bautista de las Casas   1811
Cristobal Dominguez   1813-1814
Benito Arminan, Mariano Varela, Ignacio Perez,
    Manuel Pardo   1814-1817
Antonio Maria Martinez   1817-1822
Jose Felix Trespalacios   1822-1823
Luciano Garcia   1823

MEXICAN PERIOD

Rafael Gonzales   1824-1826
Victor Blanco   1826-1827
Jose Maria Viesca   1827-1831
Jose Maria Letona   1831-1832
Juan Martin Veramendi   1832-1833
Juan Jose Elguezabal   1834-1835
Agustin Viesca   1835
Ramon Musquiz   1835

PERIOD OF THE REPUBLIC

Henry Smith   1835-1836
David Gouverneur Burnet   1836
Sam Houston   1836-1838, 1841-1844

Mirabeau Buonaparte Lamar   1838-1841
Anson Jones   1844-1846

STATE PERIOD

James Pinckney Henderson   1846-1847
George T. Wood   1847-1849
Peter Hansborough Bell   1849-1853
James Wilson Henderson   1853
Elisha Marshall Pease   1853-1857, 1867-1869
Hardin R. Runnels   1857-1859
Sam Houston   1859-1861
Edward Clark   1861
Francis R. Lubbock   1861-1863
Pendleton Murrah   1863-1865
Andrew J. Hamilton   1865-1866
James Webb Throckmorton   1866-1867
Edmund Jackson Davis   1870-1874
Richard Coke   1874-1876
Richard B. Hubbard   1876-1879
Oran M. Roberts   1879-1883
John Ireland   1883-1887
Lawrence Sullivan Ross   1887-1891
James Stephen Hogg   1891-1895
Charles A. Culberson   1895-1899
Joseph Draper Sayers   1899-1903
Samuel Willis Tucker Lanham   1903-1907
Thomas Mitchell Campbell   1907-1911
Oscar Branch Colquitt   1911-1915
James E. Ferguson   1915-1917
William P. Hobby   1917-1921
Pat M. Neff   1921-1925
Miriam A. Ferguson   1925-1927, 1933-1935
Dan Moody   1927-1931

Ross S. Sterling	1931-1933
James V. Allred	1935-1939
W. Lee O'Daniel	1939-1941
Coke R. Stevenson	1941-1947
Beauford Halbert Jester	1947-1949
Allan Shivers	1949-1957
Price Daniel	1957-1963
John B. Connally	1963-1969
Preston Smith	1969-1973
Dolph Briscoe, Jr.	1973-

Bibliography

This is a selected bibliography. Contemporary newspaper reports, letters, and interviews are not listed, and only a few of the numerous book-length biographies of governors are included. Only a few listings are made of the numerous treatments of Texas governors in the *Quarterly* of the Texas State Historical Association.

Adair, A. Garland. *A Century of Texas Governors and Capitols.* Austin: Von Boeckmann-Jones Company, 1943.

Baker, D. W. C., comp. *A Texas Scrapbook.* New York: W. S. Barnes and Company, 1875.

Bancroft, Hubert Howe. *History of the North Mexican States and Texas.* 2 vols. San Francisco: A. L. Bancroft & Company, 1886.

Bolton, Herbert Eugene. *Anthanase de Mezieres and the Louisiana-Texas Frontier, 1768-1780.* 2 vols. Cleveland: Arthur H. Clark Company, 1914.

————. *Texas in the Middle Eighteenth Century.* Berkeley: University of California Press, 1915.

Bolton, Paul. *Governors of Texas.* Corpus Christi: Corpus Christi Caller Times, 1947.

Bonilla, Antonio. "Brief Compendium of the Events Which Have Occurred in the Province of Texas ... Written in 1772." Translated by Elizabeth Howard West. Texas State Historical Association *Quarterly*, 8 (July, 1904), 9-72.

Brown, John Henry. *History of Texas, from 1685 to 1892.* Saint Louis: L. E. Daniell, 1892.

Castaneda, Carlos. *Our Catholic Heritage in Texas*. 7 vols. Austin: Von Boeckmann-Jones Company, 1936-1950.

Cotner, Robert Crawford. *James Stephen Hogg*. Austin: University of Texas Press, 1959.

Current Biography Yearbook. New York: H. W. Wilson Company, 1940-.

Daniell, L. E. *Texas: The Country and Its Men*. (Apparently published by the author, n.d.)

Day, Donald, and Harry Hubert Ullom, eds. *The Autobiography of Sam Houston*. Norman: University of Oklahoma Press, 1954.

DeShields, James T. *They Sat in High Places*. San Antonio: Naylor Company, 1940.

Dictionary of American Biography. New York: Charles Scribner's Sons, 1928-.

Fitzgerald, Hugh Nugent. *Governors I Have Known*. Austin: Austin American Statesman, 1927.

Gambrell, Herbert. *Anson Jones: The Last President of Texas*. Garden City: Doubleday and Company, 1948.

Garrett, Julia Kathryn. *Green Flag over Texas*. New York and Dallas: Jenkins Publishing Company, 1969.

Graham, Philip. *Thc Life and Poems of Mirabeau B. Lamar*. Chapel Hill: University of North Carolina Press, 1938.

James, Marquis. *The Raven: A Biography of Sam Houston*. New York: Blue Ribbon Books, 1929.

Johnson, Frank W. *A History of Texas and Texans*. Vol. 1. Chicago and New York: American Historical Society, 1914.

Kittrell, Norman G. *Governors Who Have Been and Other Public Men of Texas*. Houston: Dealy-Adey-Elgin Company, 1921.

Moore, Walter B. *Governors of Texas*. Dallas: Dallas Morning News, n.d.

Morphis, J. M. *History of Texas*. New York: United States Publishing Company, 1874.

Phares, Ross. *Cavalier in the Wilderness: The Story of the Explorer and Trader, Louis Juchereau de St. Denis*. Baton Rouge: Louisiana State University Press, 1952.

Pichardo, Jose Antonio. *Pichardo's Treatise on the Limits of Louisiana and Texas*. . . . Translated by Charles Wilson Hackett. 4 vols. Austin: University of Texas Press, 1931-1946.

Robles, Vito Alessio. *Coahuila y Texas desde la Consumacion de la Independencia hasta el Tratado de Paz de Guadalupe Hidalgo*. 2 vols. Mexico City, 1945.

———. *Coahuila y Texas en la Epoca Colonial*. Mexico City, 1938.

Smith, W. Roy. "The Quarrel between Governor Smith and the Council of the Provisional Government of the Republic." Texas State Historical Association *Quarterly*, 5 (1901-1902), 269-346.

Texas Parade, January, 1971, pp. 22-26; January, 1973, pp. 24-28.

Webb, Walter Prescott. *The Texas Rangers*. Boston and New York: Houghton Mifflin Company, 1935.

———, and H. Bailey Carroll, eds. *The Handbook of Texas*. 2 vols. Austin: Texas State Historical Association, 1952.

Weddle, Robert S. *Wilderness Manhunt: The Spanish Search for La Salle*. Austin: University of Texas Press, 1973.

Who's Who in America. Chicago: Marquis, 1899-.

Who's Who in the South and Southwest. Chicago: Marquis, 1947-.

Yoakum, H. *History of Texas*. 2 vols. New York: Redfield, 1855.

Index